RAW MIND

VOLUME I

GROWING PAINS
AN UPLIFTING DIRECTIVE

EVAN MCMILLAN

DIVINE GRIND

#9848635 #98435763

Houston, Texas

RAW MIND
VOLUME I
Growing Pains
AN UPLIFTING DIRECTIVE

© 2020 Evan McMillan

Special thanks to Houghton Harcourt Mifflin for granting permission to reprint an excerpt by Anaïs Nin in The Diary of Anaïs Nin, Vol. 4: 1944–1947, ed. Gunther Stuhlmann (New York: Harcourt Brace Jovanovich, 1971).

This book is protected under the copyright laws of the United States of America. Any reproduction or other unauthorized use of the material herein is prohibited without the expresswritten permission of the author.

For permission requests, contact the publisher:
Divine Grind
Houston, Texas

Printed in the United States of America

ISBN: 978-1-7360666-0-7
E-book ISBN: 978-1-7360666-1-4
Library of Congress Control Number: 2020921598

Contents

Introduction xiii
The Gardener xiv

PART I: THE DIAGNOSIS 1

   1. Awareness 3
      Pain 5
      Outlaw 8
      Mentality 9
      Money Whipped 12
      Greed 14
      Deceitful 16
      After Dark 18
      Abuse 20
      Addiction 21
      Red Lights 22

   2. In Transition 25
      Dodging Darkness 27
      Smoke 29
      Over-Ambitious 31
      Housekeeping 33
      Second Thoughts 34
      Mistakes 36

   3. The Struggle 38
      Let Me Breathe 40
      Vent 44
      To Protect and Serve 46
      Ignorant 48
      Broken Rules 50
      Death to Justice 52
      Suspecting Suspect 53
      Show Me, Don't Tell Me 55
      Forgotten 57
      Confined 58

Memorial 60

4. Unintended 63
    The Real Her 65
    Payback..67
    Revenge 69
    Guilty..71
    Ghost of Love..73
    Listen..75
    Never Learn 79

5. Dysfunction 81
    Cold Heart 83
    Rebound...85
    Covers...87
    Abusive 89
    Spiteful..90
    Snake...92
    Scissors 93
    Stage Left...96

6. Worth.. 98
    Crush..100
    Her Pool 102
    Selfish Gifts...103
    Unfair Exchange 105
    Losing What I Never Had.............................107

7. Growth 110
    Misery...112
    My Ways...113
    Dwelling...114
    Missing My Flight 116
    Chasing the Runner...117
    The Climb 119
    Weakness..121
    Better...122

To See Destiny..125

PART II: THE PRESCRIPTION 127

8. The Monster 129
    Malice 131
    Losing It 133
    Ulterior 135
    Checks 137
    Retaliation 139
    Suicide Note 142
    My Monster 144

9. To Tame the Monster 147
    Me vs. Me 149
    Suicidal Killer 151
    Younger Me 153
    Survivor 155
    Bittersweets 156
    Scars 158
    Entitled 159

    Thanks to You 162

10. Mental Work 165
    Get Up 167
    Image 169
    Swan 171
    Philosophy 173
    Suppressors 175
    Talk 176
    Heart 178
    Meant 179

    Perfection 181

11. Overcoming 184
    Remember Me? 186

Limits 188
　　　Tease..189
　　　Without You 190
　　　My Fly-By Bye 192

12. Love Life.. 195
　　　Love Songs 197
　　　New Love..198
　　　Losing Love..200
　　　Indescribable 201
　　　Values 202

13. The Blessing and the Curse............. 204
　　　Fallen Star 206
　　　Fall from Grace..................................207
　　　Verdict 209
　　　In My Shoes.......................................213
　　　Bible Thumper 214
　　　Abandoned 215
　　　Your Spoiled Desire..........................216

14. Free Me 219
　　　Humbled 221
　　　Playing With Him 223
　　　I Owe You One 224
　　　Rededicate 225
　　　Faith of Faith.....................................227
　　　Growing...230

15. Resolutions 232
　　　In the Garden....................................234
　　　Happiness 236
　　　Rain 237
　　　Better Days..238
　　　Endings 241

A Note From the Author 242
About the Author..244

GLORY TO GOD

Nothing of true meaning and
Absolute fulfillment
Can be done apart from
The Almighty
GOD IS MY POWER

He, in whose image we were created
Said, "Let it be," and it was…
It still is.
This is the power we must seek
To unearth from within this dirt.

For my mother
My angel
Here since the beginning
There through it all

*"We do not grow absolutely, chronologically.
We grow sometimes in one dimension, and not in another; unevenly.
We grow partially. We are relative.
We are mature in one realm, childish in another.
The past, present, and future mingle and pull us backward, forward,
or fix us in the present."*

– THE DIARY OF ANAÏS NIN, VOL. 4: 1944–1947

Introduction
#7815987 #78159876

> This is not to teach you, but you can learn.
> This is not to change you, but you can gain perspective.
> This may not show you the way, but I hope you find it.
> I'm not saying everything will be alright,
> but I hope you believe it will be.

You are not alone.

You with those thoughts that you don't ever share, the pain that you pretend you don't feel. You with the missing piece you try to cover up—that part you hide to forget—so you can act like you never cared.

We've all been there. I've been there. That's why these words are given to you. On the muddy climb toward the light, my heart lies bare before your eyes. My life before the diagnosis; my life with the prescription.

You'll see some good, some bad, and some ugly. In this volume, *Growing Pains,* there's a whole lot of ugly. It's a wonder how the ugliness holds so much of our attention when there is so much beauty in this world. We allow the ugliness to soak in, soak into us. Yet it's a trap. It's a lie. Just as the lies deform the thoughts of your mind, they deform the core of your heart. This ugliness is like a stain—a deep stain.

My stain was once deeper, but it was only a stain. A mere stain on a heart that is still capable. Capable, full of potential, still beautiful. I am no garment to be tossed away, discarded, rendered useless because of a stain. This is what makes our world beautiful: these hearts that are perfectly imperfect. These unique beauty marks.

In these pages, the blood of my heart is as the ink of my pen. There were no brainstorms, no tidy paths, no trying to say the right thing. It's pure expression, spilling out as my life unfolds. This was not on purpose, but this is my purpose.

This is *RAW MIND.*

The Gardener

What seeds are planted, what plants will grow
Where the seeds are planted
Is from where the plants will grow
Add water, show them the light
Or the seeds will go unnoticed underneath the surface
And will not bear fruit
The fruits of plants contain seeds
A future harvest
Exponential growth
May your plant become an orchard

Keep count of what you have gained
But don't only count for what you can gain
Greed is a wild fire
Greed will burn down your orchard
Don't sell all your fruit,
Leaving yourself without seeds
Don't lose all to gain all
Believe you will gain in respect for time
In respect for the orchard you have grown

Seeds need to breathe
Seeds are choked by weeds
Shoots for no fruit
Pay attention to the leaves
Those sprouts you doubt
Sprouts you don't know about
See what doesn't belong
And don't let it be long

Take care of your orchard
Take care of your seeds,
They will take care of you
Be loyal to your ideal
Be loyal to those loyal

Profits are the gifts of seeds
Currency is a mere tool
A tool of trade, only a representation of worth
Not worth itself

Worth is life
Worth may be measured by currency
But it is worth that brings forth wealth
Currency has no life of its own
Lifeless
Needing life to be relevant

Seeds are life
The bearers of life
The plant that becomes is the essence of life
The fruit is the gift of life
The gift can be, or can become any gift necessary
This provides the illusion
Where the fruit is the object of worth

But underestimated is the seed
At the core of the fruit
The seed, of superior worthiness
As vulnerable as it may seem by its size
And as irrelevant as it may seem by its humbled presence
By its hidden glory
The seed has absolute Power

May your seed become an orchard!

THE DIAGNOSIS

1.

Awareness

#5926827 #59248972

Darkness is a pit I was pushed into
Until I remembered how I got here
I remember how I closed my eyes
Because the light was too bright
Against these mirrors that were held before me
Reflecting my flaws
The glare chased me where
I can open my eyes and don't have to see
Until my eyes adjust and I must

Now I see darkness is a pit I fell into
Without the light to guide me
This new day, without the night to hide me
In the foggy mirrors that blind me
Within the dimensions that confine me
I finally find me
Lost in pain

It's in our nature to grow.

As soon as we are born, we begin growing. Life begins with growth. Life is growth, ever-changing, ever-expanding. As long as we are growing, we are moving forward in life, so as long as we are moving forward, we should be growing. Time stops for no one. Time is designed in a way that forces us to move forward. We must move forward, but as we do, we realize something else: growth inevitably faces resistance.

Not all of us are aware of the exact nature of resistance, and this mystery is its weapon. Perhaps it is introduced into our lives by people, events, negative thoughts—or not enough thought. Regardless, when shrouded in mystery, resistance can take destructive forms, such as temptation, fear, discouragement, or doubt. Each of us faces different forms of resistance and experience different forms of corresponding pain. In all its destructive forms, resistance opposes the flow of life, hinders the path to our desired destiny.

However, resistance loses its power over us once we gain understanding of its nature. The truth is that there is no mystery. Its only true weapon, then, is our ignorance.

We each have our own unique ways that we perceive, feel, and identify pain. Becoming aware of our relation to pain is part of the process of growth. It is the beginning to learning to adapt, handle, and overcome adversity. In awakening to this truth, we have the opportunity to move forward with a new strength, defeating every form of resistance through perseverance.

As we persevere, the adverse circumstances help mold our character. As we grasp the nature of resistance, understanding how and why it affects us, we come to understand the nature of ourselves . . . once we have moved past these *Growing Pains*.

Pain

– Pills don't kill
Life, plight, losing the fight
Bills, ills, losing the will
Like the ties they begin loosing at will
When I expect them to be here
They're too busy burying love
With all my heart
I feel nothing in particular
It's everything I can't explain
Attacks in the spiritual
When no one else is listening
When my best interest isn't interesting
In their own world
How they look at me
Leaving me

Down and out
Looks at the outcast
Looking down
Look at me downcast
Look around
I try to come around
But I stay down
Looking for them to pick me up
But they just put me down
Self-inflictions
I let them bring me down
In pain

I wipe my eyes
Wet wipes
I try to put these things aside
Growing tissue
Time will heal
Until they bring down their heel

Kicking me when I'm down
Steel toes don't feel
Wishing we could feel the same
Either way
They don't feel my pain

Irritating wounds
Undressed too soon
Not addressed soon enough
It can get a little rough
Playing tough
Serious games
Goals of anythings
Nothing blocking this mirror of shame
Too many panes

In these windows of my soul
I see tension in my vision
When my friends become distant
Squinting
Are they blind to my position
Or are they only blind when they listen
To cries of lies in sighs?
Or they don't hear what they're not near
As I die of why's in bye's?
Or is this how they respond to wrong
To avoid responding to wrong wrong?
Hurtful truths
Or comfort lies
Aren't they so wise
Knowing they can't help
A man who can only help himself

I need a push
They push me away
A need to be touched in some way
My needs I won't say,
I can't say
I only want one thing

Feel
My
Pain

Outlaw

Hated by loved ones
Loved by the hated ones
Finding peace in chaos
Blending, where the lights stay off

In the light I feel off
Darkness my game
Midnight like playoffs
I'll die for the chance to be the champ
I just have to make it past the vamps

Blood money our trophy
The company for the lonely
My company makes me lonely
Home alone,
Watching out for homies

Never really homey
In the streets a home that's never really cozy
Living the fast life
Like dying the slow death
Dying for nothing
Because its killing me there's nothing left
Never, nothing right
That way always out of sight
That door they always shut
Pointing, saying I'm wrong for being out here
Looking out their window, as they draw their curtains
Blaming me for staying out here

Mentality

Robbery
It's all black to me
Do you see who's robbing me?
Someone sold my soul to poverty
A hole in me
Black holes left
To consume the whole of me

It's something in the air . . .
It might be nothing—no air
It's cold in those streets
But it's too hot in here
To breathe I fail
Is it sweat or are those tears?
Screams and wails I inhale
Is it death or is it fear?
I can't tell
Or do they fear death is near?
Or do I feel it here?

Empty echoes in the hall
Empty echoes as we fall
Back against this wall
Here I hear this empty stomach
Breaking the silence of empty thoughts
Checking to see

It's all empty!

Empty bowls, dry plates, empty boxes
Empty ice boxes
Even empty of ice
I still get a chill standing here

I see dumpster diving
In a sea of maybe
My eyes glisten
Stung by the stench of the steel coffin
I'll die before I get in
Me and my pride
We both can't fit in

Applications given and never taken
Every business I see
Shows me where I have no business to be
Up to the end of the road
To the corner I'm sold
As she sells for what I sell

Being killed by bills
My life taken from me
A percentage sold back by hell
I barely had enough to post bail
Undercover they sell the last I had to sell
Evidence that he robbed me
It's all smoke, it's dissolving
My only food
I'm still starving

When I get a full plate
My appetite makes me seem greedy
My eyes seem bigger than my stomach
My mind is stuck on needy
I can't seem to fill this empty stomach
Even though I get all needs freely
I'm still broke in spirit
So I raise it
To buy a smile
For a frown I couldn't afford to turn around

I turn around
And throw it in your face
But it's not the same one you gave me
I used to hate you couldn't love me
Now I love how you hate me
How you made me
Say I'm ignorant, I never knew money
But this is how I know money
—No Money

Money Whipped

Money all around me
From the outside looking in
She's grinning in
What I'm swimming in
But I'm actually drowning

All the money that surrounds me
Too much money around me
She looks my way
And she sees the ripple on the surface
But she still hasn't found me
I'm in too deep
And I can't see past the sea
Lost the sight of the dream
The map of the Promised Land,
The lost plan

I work just to work
Always more work
All the things I say I'd do,
To live like I have nothing to lose
And all I have to do is give it all up

It sounds so easy
But it's like saying "free yourself" to a slave
All I have to do is get out of these chains
But these chains are made of gold
Chained to foundations of diamond cornerstones
I think I see the key
But it's always just out of reach
I still reach

Out of greed
It doesn't mean I'm being freed
I can't ask for help
My only friends are slaves
Stuck in the same situation
Only around because he makes them
They are not loyal to me
They are loyal to the master
They come because he called
He keeps me close, but they don't come for me at all
They would harm me if ordered,
They would leave me to die if told
To remain in good graces
Thinking being a better slave would lead to freedom
All the while making themselves more valuable as slaves
Feeling as if you work hard enough you'll reach your goal
But he never plans to let you go

Greed

Our plays for the throne
For a kingdom for a home
To own on our own

She dances with dragons
Entangles their wings
Grounded forever, the sky her domain
Her passion will swallow any such wrath
Her eyes eat fire
Once the beast is summoned
There are those of power who fall
For the power she shows
Her beauty raised from the depths of death
That's how she will catch you in their glow

Good life, entranced
Enhanced, full days
Bright nights, the kind that never come from bright lights
A love that never sums up to satisfaction,
Only a craving for more
Maxed black credit cards of shopaholics in stores
Goodnight
Can't, knowing there's better
Can't be, but maybe if you let her
Knock down walls
Like you don't remember why they're there
Or not enough to care

She's not mean, well, not in these dreams
That make it seem like you have control
Damaged goods, deliveries of a broken soul
The blue flames she was forged in
That hell she was formed in
That art she was trained in
Capabilities she can never rein in
That reign in storms that can't be reined in
Like the wind and rain in
This queen hails
Where emptiness dwells

Where a need swells
Bad apples digested by this snow-white desert
When you see those blizzards in her eyes
When you're hypnotized
Frozen in her presence
Her influence
The becoming of a cold heart

Deceitful

Temptation
Satanic manipulation
Using me
Against me
How my desires influence me
To chase after what I don't need
A life I don't lead
To be persuaded to want
What is placed in the trap
Unaware of the hunt

Caught up in distracting things
Never getting enough of the small stuff
Not looking at the bigger picture
What you see is what you get
What did I even see?
What did I miss?
Is everything given a gift?

She beckons me with a hiss
Her piercing eyes, her luscious lips
She grabs my hand, I don't resist

She walks, and I trip
She walks, but I slip
She promises me with her hips
Everything on my list

She moves with a twist
I go low as she dips
I can't stop once I start
I look up, and we've gone so far
Gone so long it's starting to get dark
It's starting on my heart

Her place is dark like a cave
The rooms dark like the shade
On her black bed she lays,
Black lingerie

I'm summoned by her dark gaze
I can't look away
I'm in before I'm in
My shadow dimming as it dims
He becomes part of me
Or I become part of him
Drawing him in
Or he draws me
Shading in that darkened grin
As her lips draw me to them
Her kiss, sweet as SIN

After Dark

All these late nights
I'm rolling right through the red lights
They barely get a glimpse of my taillights
I'm a ghost to the green eye
I ride all night, until I see that pale light
I hide as the sun's passing by
The smoke is so bright in this stale night
But it's so gray in the light
My mind is only clear when I stay out of sight
But the only thing clear is to stay out of their sights
Clammy hands, moist guns
Safety a void with quick thumbs
Risks for quick funds
These quick trips feel like long ones

Regardless of the consequences
I'm out here, open for all business
I board her swaying ship for the shipment
Disregarding the consequences, the tempests
The temptress

She can never be my wife
But I still give my life to this night
Something's amiss, but I dismiss it
Something like bliss describes her kisses
It's something like love
But not quite a commitment
But we go the distance
She says to never bring a witness
True feelings I don't witness,
I'm too distant

Rolling stops past the stop signs
I don't see the signs, I've lost myself
So that's why
In this mind there's not a care what a cop finds
Losing myself in pursuit of my pursuer
Street lights leading to hell, catching glimpses of red tails
As night lays across these empty highways
I become a fast lane mover
All these different lanes,
But I'm not surprised that I choose her

I like her because she says she loves me
But she hates that I confuse her
The way I do her, she says I use her
Now she's the one who confuses
What would I do with you if you were useless?
Cook up sins, and give me a peep show
Feed me lies, and then stroke my ego
Make me money, make me a hero

But I can't save myself
Because I'm the victim
Of a vixen
I've been lured in
These streets I'm in
This game I'm in
—This siren

Abuse

I bring myself to
Groaning as I drag
Taking out the trash
Bottles clinking in the bag
A glass choir sings a chorus
Testimonies corroborated
With the butts in the dash
Dotting the ash like the crumbs in my lash

Sleep on top of sleep
Like freak on top of freak
Down from my peak
The white caps of the mountain of my tweak

That place I hate to leave
Like a love that's not good for me
Evidence, like those telling tattoos
Hidden by the sleeve
Shame I look past, still I always see
Her lips tattooed on my skin
Show how deep she went, how deep she got me
They say I need treatment from her mistreatment
I don't see my weakness

Now so frequent
When I need it, when I get it
Not always in the same sequence
And make-believe medicine
Popping props for my plays
Got into a wreck, said it was a phase
I was just setting the stage

Addiction

That tall wall you raised
Like a fence it fell
The attack of the itch
When you give up an inch
Milestones of defenses fail
Kimbers quiver as timbers shiver
War cries that are cowardly yells
Black sails carried by whispering winds
Like quiet storms, those death hails
Reaching shore, foundations break
Rolling waves from their massive wake

Plunging into red rivers
You can only scratch the surface
Where they infiltrate, into the vessels of life's heartbeat
Pirates venture in the deep
The captain hooks
Then by the lines they sink

Avoiding the mirror, facing the sink
Like bad breath, and creepy winks make you shrink
Back
In back seats in your best in fleet
Where your pride makes you weak
Making things that you cannot let one see
That make things you have to make

Lying
On your deathbed telling them you feel so great
Lying in an unmarked grave
There's no difference
Despite the tombstone that you'll never make

Red Lights

From the darkness of the valleys of alleys
Seeing the tops of mountains bathed in moonlight
Like high rises and city lights
Looking from the lowest point
Pointing toward the highest place
The only way I get a smile on this face

I've always dreamed to reach a height
To see the world in a different light
To be so close to the stars
Up there there's probably never night
To be in a place where they can't turn off your lights

But I'm tired already
It takes too much time
I thought I'd be there already
It takes too much to climb
I look up and realize I'm not ready
I never thought hiking would be so tough
All this stuff I have to carry
I've had enough
But looking down scares me

The road up the mountain is rough
And it's too long
Thinking there should be a shortcut
I tried to lay a new road using my own stuff
I wish I could've looked beyond time
I was blind, being pushed from behind
My past and all those heavy thoughts pushing my mind
To rush to construct what impatience chanted
My head was tilted from the weight,
I couldn't take the wait
My highways ended up slanted

Stressed supports
My supports were stresses
I just ended up falling off the cliff
Like the coyote that chases something he never catches

My dreams never came
Life made me restless
Never had a rest
Fell asleep at the intersection

The green light finally shows
As I have my eyes closed
Missing my opportunity

I finally open my eyes
Yellow lights warn me
No,
I still feel I have to go
Even though I know what comes next
So why am I perplexed?

Now I look at the damage as I scratch my head
My life's a total wreck!

AWARENESS
knowledge that something is happening or exists

2.

In Transition
#8969241 #89621765

My destructive lifestyle pacifies my pain
I see it must change
I see I don't change
I chase money out of fear of being broke
I don't trust anyone because of fear of being let down
I overcompensate in dominance to conquer my weaknesses
And I fear becoming vulnerable
All these fears derive from pre-existing pain
So I am not being healed
I am just being distracted

I feed pain
So I don't have to feel it feed on me
I hurt myself so it won't hurt me
This I don't realize
This pain is so consuming
It has spread from the areas from which it originated
I eventually look up and see
This pain has become so powerful
It has taken control of my whole life

It is time I take it back

Everyone has experienced growing pains. We may face heartbreak, feelings of loneliness, unworthiness, trauma, and abuse or addiction. It's in how we respond to the pain that we differ. Some of us display it publicly; some deal with it privately. Some hold it in until they explode.

At the core of our responses is evidence of whether or not we grasp the role of pain in growth. There are those who know that pain is necessary to grow. Then there are those who get stuck in the pain, crippled by it, allowing it to have authority over their lives. I was once the latter, hindered by the power of pain, which was only an illusion. By acknowledging it as a powerful force, I fed it, fueled it. The more I fed it, the more it grew. The more I fueled it, the more power it retained.

To avoid yielding to this fraudulent authority, pain must be processed as part of the process of growth. For some people, this happens naturally. They have tunnel vision and focus on the light at the end. Others who are less disciplined and easily distracted need to actively process the pain. They have to constantly make an effort to remind themselves of their impetus, especially when negativity and discouragement strike. Reminding ourselves of our past victories or considering examples of content and successful people who have experienced pain and have grown from it are good motivations to keep pushing. Move forward with whatever technique that best suits you to get through the pain.

The goal is to recognize the role of pain in growing and adapting. Life is about evolution. Mentally and spiritually, we have to adapt moment to moment, year to year. Despite our past responses to pain, it is possible to experience power over our circumstances when we realign ourselves with a positive direction. And each time we experience our power over circumstance, we get better, stronger, and wiser. Through faith, hope, and love, we emerge from pain, giving way to growth. As we begin to acknowledge and use our power, we begin to identify the most effective ways to wield this power. Eventually, executing this knowledge will be habitual. When it becomes second nature to us, we will have evolved . . . We must keep evolving.

Dodging Darkness

I woke up in a nightmare
Now my dreams fade away, and the night stares
I look away
I look this way, and that
I'll accept anything for escape
This is why I never escape
Panicked breaths
The death I exhale
Only because of the need to inhale
There's nothing but greed in the air
To be filthy rich
This stench that sticks
How do I leave this place I'm in?
It has become a part of me
The cloud I was on
It's on me
This lingering fog
This choking smog

Even with day light my day's dark
Even though my eyes stay bright, it stays dark
Can you see what I can't see?
The good in me does no good for me
I could be free, but I couldn't leave
It would be, but it wouldn't be

What should be, I wouldn't see
Until I couldn't see
Through this darkness that shouldn't be
With this bright light and these light rays
With the sun up, which leaves
But leaves the moon corrupt
When the light shows, so do shadows
When it becomes dark they become you
When you don't see what is in you
But you feel

He won't leave, I must leave him
This desire is a fire
And as it grows it glows
And then he shows, he won't go though
He still follows
Dodging darkness

Light lightens my load
Must not become darkened
I must light the night
My fright my might
My plight my sight
I must see to see
What resides in what it hides
—To dodge darkness

Smoke

The smoke 'n mirrors
The smoke is so much clearer
Clearing my mind
As I erase what I find
I find I have the power to erase time
Times too

Two-timing, two-faced, facetime
Smoke 'n mirrors
Severing direct lines
Smoking in the mirror
Out of touch with my enemies
The smoke is so much clearer
But somehow they still get to me
Absorbed in my misery
But I can't see myself killing me
As I hold it all in
Pulling a shotgun to my head

All I want is smoke
I close my eyes,
Waiting to be taken away
Bullets and lies
I want the smoke
I can't see
What it separates me from
All I see is that it separates for me
When the smoke clears

When God calls
And Satan hears
And interrupts
But this double-edged sword still
Takes me out
This double-mind
Divided

Separated from the hate
If it wasn't for that grace
I would've never found love
The type that only comes from above

All forgotten in a cell

Re-enter into hell
No wonder I can't hear him that well
Distraction
Or is it that I don't listen too well
Reaction
Revenge dwells in the soul of an unavenged male
My pride pushes for retaliation
Demons push upon me invitations
Life by a gun that encourages me to die blazing

In the midst of the same smoke
That eats souls but always feeds yours
That fattened calf, your sacrifice
For a street life under street lights
That shine on blood diamonds
And these rocks don't go in a peace pipe
Let them inhale that death wish
Then I take this stress hit
I say it's to ease my mind
But it's to keep me blind

Over-Ambitious

I was blind,
See, I saw I was fine
I never saw proof
To see I was playing games
With life I never chose truth
The dare devil

Feeling like a superhero
Dying for savings
Motivations by sayings
The sky's the limit
Never had an idol,
Distracted, distractions
I looked up to the moon and stars
To see it all
My eyes so big,
I went too far for the shoes and cars

Luxuries
That cost too much
Lavish
How did I waste so much?
I gave my all
I paid so much
The wrong investments
Indebted, to my sins
Those interests that seem to never end
A percentage of stress on the pen
The ink skips lines…

To feel a pause
To redirect my cause
Better effects to better affect
To never neglect, only always neglect
Love for money
True and false
It's really trading love for money

Truth
The false succumbs to
Fallen strength, built upon earth that quakes
Face what the ground runs to
Faster than you brought yourself up
Faster than your impatience
—Your foundations

Housekeeping

This party is out of hand
I pray and take a stand
People slip and fall
The blind spill the wine
They don't see the rest
The deaf gets what's left
They don't hear the cries for help
Wisdom takes time
And it will take a while to clean this mess
Fools brag of their knowledge
But whine when they see the test
I just do my best

The lights flicker
As the storm whispers
The horseman's reins spur whickers
As the dark prince snickers
When I bite off more than I can chew
But I'm a fat boy at heart
Eventually, I'll get through

Thieves in the garden
Demons in my backyard
Now I hear, the horn's growing
Headlights swinging my way
Angels pulling in the driveway
The doorbell rings away
Like the jingle of the chains that keep me away
So close, but so far away

I think of the key I keep in the secret place
How when you really need it, it's never there
Then the door creaks and peace flows like creeks
I'm so glad he keeps a spare

Second Thoughts

Head first into whatever
Hard times come, do they make me hardheaded?
How sudden storms appear in perfect weather
Bets placed statistically better
What are the odds?

How it feels to go against the odds
Eyes on the prize, how you look once you've lost
Hardheaded, face in palms
The bottom flattened against your soft cheeks

Flatten out those paper balls
Wrinkles in between the lines
Squinting to see squiggles of scribbles
The barely wake of the drunken pencil
Wake up to the drizzle
Her tears exploding from the lead of wooden missiles
Looking over the aftermath
Absorbing the magnitude of consequences
Impulsiveness, uncalculated decisions
Reverse engineer emotions
Like closing your eyes to focus

Like the ice that survives
Perseverance from the fire that burns my throat
Melting my anxiety
As it blurs my vision
The key in my back
But without you, I could never find my ignition
What drives me, and everything I let pass
So passive
Aggressive in your method, to not be neglected
Uncontrolled expressions, so unaware
The need to be expressive

Unerased, artful mistakes, no retakes
Impressions forever made
Soft lines on hard surfaces
Like wood grain, like good pain
Afterthoughts, like sawdust
Like sandpaper
Like a do-over
Just to smooth it over

Mistakes

Full of knowledge that doesn't work
Transferred wisdom that does not reach
Failures, only that truly teach
Pain of scars, those marks that can't be erased
Once the pain fades memories remain
The permanence worse than pain

The stain you wipe, then smudge, then spread
Those reminders by the third eye glancing back
When you can't look away fast enough
Those photographs you can't untake
How negatives can't be erased

Fuel for the true picture to develop
Greater minds rising through tough times
Conditioned in conditions
Where the knowledge works out
Once the wisdom has stretched
Is it bad, what's not good?
For better for worse is best
Only divorce regrets
Walking down the aisle of life
To live with it

TRANSITION
a condition or situation in life undergoing a process that is to bring forth change

3.

The Struggle
#5942152 #59462916

To feel so much hate,
How can I show love?
I'm consumed in pain
I can give nothing else
No one cares for my life
How can I be expected to care for another?
I give others too much control over my life;
I don't want to be the effect of another's cause
I want to have my own cause
No one can free me
But me
No one can hold me back
But me

In the struggle, in this pain, we wonder, "How long will this process take us? How far will we push it? How far will we let it push us?"

We are strong, but sometimes we allow our strength to be manipulated into weakness. We have so much love, but sometimes we let hate intrude. In the midst of this pain, having inherited this fiercely selfish will to survive, it seems we are set up to fail. With the enemy advancing, why would you or I turn our weapons against our fellow soldiers? Why would we help them kill us?

Yet we are pushed to push through without the chance to think it through. In the moment, it doesn't matter what it brings us to. It doesn't seem like anybody cares, because they are just as consumed with pain and focused on survival themselves. In the moment, you may think, "Who can matter but me?" And how can you be blamed?

But you are blamed. Life may feel unfair, but only you and I are responsible for ourselves. Our lives are the result of our thoughts and our actions.

So don't see what they see. No longer see what they want you to see. See what you want to be, to be what you want to see. Do not be an effect to another's cause. Take control of your life, of your future, of your destiny. You have a responsibility.

Don't let us down.

Let Me Breathe

Gasping . . .
This struggle
Everyday,
I exercise this muscle
I feel your long arm tighten
Bring it on

You expect me to stay unresponsive
I respond
Wonder why I fight a losing fight?
For my life!
You are not that strong
My heart is still strong
Even after my lungs are gone

I can't breathe
See,
How I have to take a knee
I close my eyes and beg for peace
When God doesn't hear my plea,
Or his servants just don't agree

These killers never flee
Instead they all flock to me
Their sport, these stats
The in sync of the report
Like hunters surround the downed buck
They crowd a claustrophobic
My suffocation

I had a dream . . .
I couldn't breathe

I wake up
I can't breathe
Grasping, gasping

My fight for a breath
My forced desperation
For what I have left

Strangulation, clawing at invisible hands
I'm choking on your air
This poison on my tongue
Regurgitation
This exhale comes out like a cough
Like suppressed shots
Sudden chaos
But surely it was developed way off
In the night
Way before social media became a light
My bruised, bloody, broken fists
Have been
All out of fight
I still fight

I'm a mute against a mic
Bullhorns that never forewarn
Only justify injustice
How can you explain why
I can't obtain oxygen on earth's surface?
I didn't know to claim air I need a deed
I can't buy
I can't breathe

I can't breathe
I can't scream
I can't yell
No one sees
There are no riots in the streets
They're just tears down my cheeks
I set a fire, an S.O.S.
Can't you see?

This is not aggression,
This is pain in expression
If I'm the hero's enemy,
Who saves me?
I'm in danger
This is fear, this isn't anger
This is desperation, this isn't rage
This is suffocation
Strangulation
I'm thrashing against this noose
That appears loose,
But it never changed
Though there are times
When the rare wind blows in
And it sways
So I just keep on pushing
And pray that it frays
I don't see another way, I can't see
My mind isn't clear
What do I think? I don't think
I can't think
I can't breathe

To close my eyes
And hold my breath
Until I'm freed
But I won't hold my breath
For you
I can see
You won't free me
To force you to
Hold court in the streets

Still wheezing, but still willing
Wielding this voice
This small voice of mine
Is but a whisper
But collectively
Its reality is deep
My weapon of choice, my exchange
Shooting for peace

All I want is to be me
All I want is life
All I want is to matter

All I want is to be free
My peace treaty

Let
Me
Breathe

Vent

In this red rage
I won't be distracted
To be beaten
Into eyes showing black and blue
Fractions of officers are only a fraction
Systemic
This is systematic
Bureaucratic, stealth
Enigmatic

Organization
Against a whole race of humans
Organized oppression
Organized crime
Crimes you legit
You tyrant

I'm sick
And tired
Of being sick and tired
I'm tired of eating tears
And nightsticks
And bullets
And sentences without words
Gibberish unheard in the majority's suburb

New to the World News
News to the world stage
Watching me take this knee
But I'm not new to this
I'm used to this
Justice that isn't just
My heart left on ice

These are just examples that you've given us
I was raised with little air
You've been refining stuff that's polluting us
All my life I could barely breathe
Restrained by the hate you've given us

To obey those who hate me
I'm tired of submitting to your crooked cuffs
There's something stuffed up your blue sleeve
When I point at it
You point at me
I grab it and you point at me
Like I have it
You put it on me
No accountability
No responsibility

I respond with humility
And you kill me
So I respond with a little more dignity
You're still killing me!
I can't stop you from killing me!
It's killing me!
How can I get you to feel what I feel?
You don't feel me!
Who will avenge me?
Revenge is my mood now
It may be the opposite of healing me
But, so what?
If you're killing me
Nothing to lose

—This is how you make me feel

To Protect and Serve

Flashing lights, must be Christmas
Gifts of grief and pain
Unwrap the whip for the new slave

Why can't I just get a ticket?
Why must you search?
If I did have a gun, why would you be someone I'd hurt
Yes, sir, I know I'm too young to be in possession of this weapon
But sir, I live in the jungle
The lions, tigers, and bears don't care
I've seen them slaughter boys much younger
It's only for defense
I haven't robbed anyone, and I'm not an assassin on a hit
But sir, may I ask why you have one on your hip?

Yes, sir, those are drugs, but I haven't eaten in a week
And I have younger siblings to feed
No, sir,
You took my only parent from me
Yes, sir, I understand
But sir, I apply for five jobs a week, been doing that for 55 weeks
Do you realize you can die if you don't eat?
Have you ever been so hungry
That it feels like it's on you that you feed,
Your stomach on a rampage,
And you can't save yourself from its teeth?
And if you took me to jail, how would that help?
Yes, sir, I understand laws
But shouldn't somebody help a man with no help
I see your pins boasting
Implications of you making donations abroad,
While a fellow native of your nation starves
The same ones you watch daily, patrolling from your car

Waiting for a chance to make it harder
For those who have it hard
Yes, sir, I'm getting out of the car, I'm just nervous
Sir, you don't have to push me that hard

Face down, stomped into the ground, tossed around
Your yells drown my thoughts, as I'm dragged as you walk
Before I can tell you, I'm glad we had this talk

Ignorant

You skip school
So you never learn from your teachers
But you can't skip the lessons of life
The world is going to teach you
Caught up by the world
Who is going to free you?
Police don't restrain you
And you must release you

They shouldn't think what they think
Stereotypes you allow them to make
They see the hand to hand everyday
Remember, before they even gave chase
You ran away

Now you're tired of this life
Because you can't sleep at night
Feeling like you're always in the dark
Even underneath the street light
Reaping paranoia
All the self-destruction that you sow
And all the self-destruction that you sold
One of the many ways you bring destruction on your own
Hair triggers for nerves
Gun shots for words
What's worse,
Giving your life for a piece of green paper,
Or that you don't know what your life's worth?

You show off to impress your broke neighbors on section-eight
Spending all your money to show them what you make or made
No job, so how are you getting paid?
New car, big flashy wheels
One hundred thousand dollar signs
One hundred thousand snitches
Telling them to come take you away

Knowing that they'll catch you one day
Then you'll do the same thing
Expecting different destinations
From the same way
Ending up in the same place
And you accept the street credit for all these things
So how can you still give "the white man" the blame?

And the police don't have to know you by name
How can they not notice you with that paint?
Sun dancing off of the gloss
You want attention
That's exactly what you got
But he doesn't see your dark skin
He can't even see inside
Your tint is past illegal
Then he pulls you over
To inform you about your windows, or to warn you
That's when he smells the odor
In the a/c sweating
Because you have dope and guns in that hot ass car
And you have no license or registration
And as you're on the way to the station
You got the nerve to say it's because he's being racist

Broken Rules

How is it an offense when you're running the offense?
How are your aggressive tactics a defense?
When I'm hiding from you only because I stole that food
Because I don't have food
When that dude took millions from schools to buy car #102
That he probably won't even use
Oh, you two must be cool, you play golf with him too?
Are you stealing too? Well, you dress like him too
You say since he gave me a ride, I sell drugs too
It's a long walk from school
Is it true or is it true?
Since we both cock our hats, I have a pistol cocked too?

If you protect, if you defend, then why must I have a defense?
Just like we are not the same, we all are not the same
I wish I didn't have to defend myself with an offense
But I don't wish to offend, I only wish to defend
See, you never hear I shot from fear of being shot
Because a glock looks like a glock
And it looks just like your glock
But you can't hear over your shots

Aggression YOUR lesson taught to my KIND
Untamed in your attempt to tame what you claim is untamed
Attempts to validate your claim only aggravates my pain
You despise with your eyes
Your anger, my cries
You advertise the truth with lies
Consumed to confine
To confuse to define
Something undefined, something unconfined
People, different people!
Crimes are committed by your people and mine
Righteousness is found in your people and mine
Which makes both sides equal
But why should I say your people, my people

When we are all people
What is there to separate?
But you can't see straight, so you see unequal

Why when you are near, I fear the end is near?
Why do I fear what should quench my fears?
To protect and serve
If I should buy that, you'd really just sell me my tears
I pay in taxes for
Holding cells to hold my tears
And if you could hear my tears, white noise would shake the tiers
All these years, all these tears
All the fear lies from your lies of fear

It's easy to protect and serve people
When you don't see people but your people
And we don't see flaws in our friends
Are we flawed because we aren't friends?
I don't want you to take the freedom given to me
Is that what makes us enemies?

This silent war
Why do you bring this to me?
No stealth needed for
Invisible threats
For invisible death
Put in my invisible face
Someone may hear me
But no one will see me
No body, no case

The device for the Vice Lords
The cross for the Disciples
You also play the Blues
Where you drain all the Blood too
In the court you Reign
The gang that's King of Gangs

Death to Justice

Shoot me, I say, with my hand on my gun
Shoot me, I say, with my hands in the air
Shoot me! Just shoot me! I want you to shoot me!

Shoot me, I say, as I reach for my gun
Shoot me, I say, as I turn and run
Shoot me! Just shoot me! Waiting for you to shoot me!

Shoot me, I say, with the fear in my eye
Shoot me, I say, with my hands in the sky
Shoot me! Just shoot me! I've always wanted to die!

Shoot me, I say, because we're all alone
Shoot me, I say, displaying my phone
If only I could call the cops on the cops,
I still probably won't
Because they'd say I said shoot me
So they'd shoot me
And I'd get shot by them both!

Suspecting Suspect

What happens when the world stops turning around
And starts to turn upside down
What happens when you look around
And your spirit's up
Then the world turns upside down
And you're in the ground

What happens when the suspect becomes the victim
Of a suspect that can't be suspected,
But can suspect
When a suspect suspects,
Can he even suspect?

What happens when a peace officer disturbs the peace
How does the peace find release?
Even if it's just a little piece of a peace
It can't be peace, missing peace
Now how do you piece together peace
When there's nothing to replace the peace?
If a piece makes peace whole
How else do you fill the hole?
If a piece makes a hole
Where does the peace go?
How do we find peace?
You don't keep the piece you stole
Is that why you're not charged for what you owe?

In this piece you don't see such worth
This pie, this peace you desert
You serve but don't serve
But you will make someone serve
Something that they don't deserve
The ones who serve are the ones who will never serve
Praying Luke convicts you
Praying,
Because the force is with you

An enforcer that does not enforce
Is a worker that does not work
Like a judge that does not judge
False judgment is to not judge
If the law covers the land
How are there opposite sides to stand?

Enforce here, enforce there
Enforce only when you care
Enforce that, enforce this
Enforce only what you wish
The Law is only under God
You feel like you're above it,
You're wrong

Oh wait, I forgot
The world has turned upside down
You are above the law
The devil's pawn

Show Me, Don't Tell Me

Black lives matter!
Do they?
Well, obviously they can't tell
See how you throw them away

Shoot him over some shoes
Shoot him over some girl who no longer likes you
Shoot him over red, black, and blue
Or just leave him red, black, and blue
Beat him like the slave owners taught you

Kids killing and dying for blocks they never been to
Using your piece to kill
For organizations meant for unity and peace
Meant for building up the streets
That are crumbling under your feet

All about the money
Because you never had nothing
But wars cost
And on top of all that
Spending all your time risking all that time
So what is gained?
Going to war with yourself, it doesn't add up
How does that help?
A kingdom divided against itself

Shoot him at the dice game over five dollars
Because he said that was his point
You couldn't let that slide, so you pull the slide
Just to make your point
Then you went to brag about it
You were never sad about it
Then your future points to the joint
And you discharge your sentence
Just to make a point

To the guards who want to make a point
Getting under your skin
Poking at you with their points
And you become the monkey-on-a-nightstick
Just to prove a point
But only helping them prove their point
Then they go home, and they laugh at night
And you're mad about more nights in the joint

So what was your point?
To show you don't give a fuck
That's not much of a point
But it points to my point
You act like it doesn't matter, then you say it matters
Think about what you do, and think about what you say
Because you know it matters
But you don't show it matters

Who in the world would think they were wrong to take
Things that people throw away?

Forgotten

Like black lives matter
But I only see you rally behind black death
Where black is left
What about the black left

To fade to black
To the back of my mind
Like the trap I find
In my ignorance I chase this bait
Stung by a Frank face
Hook in line 'n sinking in time
Suffocated mind
The noose of this time
It stinks like a crime
Here where they hide me
The body they don't find

Manipulation by broken philosophies
Named after names with apostrophes
Though numbered not named
Freed slaves
Mentalities unchanged
Add a number to his name

Add a face to this picture
Eulogies in court
Though you never cried
As I was being buried alive
The weight of my sins
This dirt upon me
On top they throw these stones upon me
Wondering what does my Lord see
As I become invisible to me

Confined

Release me
All this cage does is deceive me
Free me
Then when I see me, I will see me
Restrained by what you make me think
Limiting me by what I know
Blinding me with what I don't

No longer will I be bound by your boundaries
No longer will I let you run circles around me
Now no ropes on the ring, now go a round with me
Now no strings on the ring, I just married me
I get what I expect of me, the best of me
You wanted to see less of me
I never knew there was more
Was never a mirror behind that door
The one you never opened

My food slid in on the floor
Came from the bottom
I never knew all fruit needs is a root
Your leftovers left me soiled
You laid the concrete on which I laid,
I never knew of soil

And now I know of thirst
All those days, I can't say I know of something worse
But you couldn't stop the leaks I now seek
The thought gives me a start
Ideal,
Putting my life together
Finding the pieces that you keep apart

STRUGGLE
strenuous effort and great desire to overcome overwhelming circumstances with inferior resources

Memorial

For those who uphold this mighty nation
For those who take a stand and make the first response
We are all unique creators
Appreciation for protecting our priceless art

Condolences
To the families of the world
Of the family of the world
The world is one great family
Even though we act like it's not so
For the brave ones we lose along the way
Loosen your prayers so they can be carried away

For the firefighters who burn inside to pave the way
For the police who are there to save, that we aren't there to save
Paramedics put their lives on the line as a spare for mine
The weight of the world on the military; all that shit they carry
Troops who are ready to die for us
Who fight for us whether wrong or right
While we safely talk down about if it's wrong or right

Don't dishonor this with politics
It's war, it's never good
We fight or die
But somehow we don't fight or die
But those who fight die
You, spoiled by the privilege to not even feel we're at war
Remember 9/11? Remember?

A dedication not only to those lost, but to those who lost
Those who sacrifice by supporting the sacrifice
Those who have shared the life that they shared
Thank you! For caring that they care even if we'll never care
Out of the understanding of the greater good
No regrets, even though it doesn't feel so great
Remaining faithful for our collective fate
Love in its absolute highest state

—Not up for debate

> Buoyancy of spirit in storms
> How we stay afloat despite overwhelming tides of life.
> To realize the held vision of silver lined shores,
> Expecting you

4.

Unintended

#6946829 #69421827

I'm blamed for pain I never intend
I'm blamed for pain I never contend
I'm blamed for pain
This life untamed
But who can I blame?

. . . I blame these poor morals
Morals keep life in check

Without intent, we create the unintentional. And without consistency, we create the inconsistent. Our circumstances, therefore, are the results of our actions—or lack of action.

In this way, we bring about resistance ourselves, whether we make the wrong choice or avoid a choice. The worst type of resistance is the kind you create yourself. To not think, to not be inspired. When we don't have a cause or our cause depends on effects, we find ourselves in emotional flux stemming from those inconsistencies in life. A lot of distress stems from us simply not using our minds, succumbing to impulses that feel good in the moment to satisfy the senses.

Take lust, for example. Lust is natural, but lust that is not checked by a disciplined mind can be detrimental and consequential. Its consummation brings momentary sexual pleasure, but at what cost?

It can lead to disease or unintended pregnancy, it can cause drama, or it can ruin relationships. It can even result in extremes such as prison or death.

We weren't meant to be simple beings, giving in to primal urges and momentary, unfulfilling pleasures that manifest negativity for ourselves and others. We are blessed with the spirit, an essence that depends on a conscious mind to protect it, to feed it, and to cultivate it. This spirit is meant to establish and sustain harmony, peace, and joy in our lives. All of our causes should reflect such values, to produce like effects. This is the significance of intent.

So be mindful about who or what you give your attention to. Be selective about where you concentrate your spiritual energy. Keep in mind the flowers you want to see blossom, and plant and water the necessary seeds accordingly. What you plant will be a plant. Be careful what you bring to life.

The Real Her

She doesn't need your trust
She doesn't want your love
For all these laws, she feels like she's above

You can feel her voice
And she whispers in your dreams
But she is never seen

But she is always seen
No cares for loyalty, not a need
She only cares to be Queen
She offers everything you dream
A satisfaction so extreme
And she is never mean
But nothing's as it seems

How does she show us all these things?
What do we owe for all these things?
She's almost always there, taking care of all your cares
She leaves a little
But she comes back for what is left
But it is not theft
You give in and she accepts

But once you say that it's not right, be prepared for a fight
All day and all night, her might becomes your plight
Her soft hands become paws
Those pretty nails become claws
Her luscious lips expose the vamp fangs resting in her jaws

You invite her in, in your touch
She's making what you must
She makes you feel you haven't had enough,

But she actually gives you too much
Until too much is not enough
That smile so easy to trust

You just addressed in love, what was dressed in love
Finally, you undress her
And now you see her . . . naked
—Lust

Payback

You want me to loan my love
Because you owe somebody
He gave you pain, that man you must pay back
Somebody hurt you, somebody has to pay
And I'll give you my all,
And all these painkillers you'll take
Hoping you can kill him with the pain

I tell you things my hormones say,
Your anger matches
Lighting up the way, as you switch and sway
I watch you heating up the stage
Everything I want to see, you show
But this is not a play
If it was I would go, go
Those hips are accelerants
My eyes ablaze
Your windows in flames
Flames dance in every pane, you dance off the pains
Your soul is on fire
Good thing I'm a fighter

I save you from yourself
Because the smoke doesn't help
Loosen up, as my lungs
Blow you away
Float on this invisible cloud
Now rain on me, darkness in your face
With those stormy eyes, now rain on me
Let it wash away every stain on me
All these dirty thoughts I need you to take away from me
Absorb my touch as I feel
Soak up all my energy
Gently killing me

But in those eyes I see overkill
In your body language is grave imagery
Erected resurrection
Look what your killer body did to me

Mixing juices, mixing our spirits
Always differently
Different angles, experimentally
Your fire so dangerous with this chemistry
With no extinguisher it's a mystery
How I put you out of your misery
But even if the heat dies down
I've left my mark
This moment will live on, branded in your memory

Revenge

Nothing feels like you
Nothing is as true
But I'm feeling . . .

There's nothing like a fool

Lost my mind over wine and food
Underneath dim lights and heavy moods
Beyond something thin, tight, and rude
That has me going mad,
But I try to hold back because this fight I'll lose
I shut doors against the slight invites
Equipped with a mean walk and some dangerous shoes
That kick the door down
The things she has to do to entice, intrude

She slides the top, she won't miss her shot
Once she puts her weapon on me, I can't refuse
Greed wraps me up, and I stroke its ego
Still making me give it up
So I also give what belongs to you

I call it theft, this inside job
Evidence left
Things that don't belong to you
Things I would never use
You say I don't care, and how can I say I do
I can only stare into nowhere as you accuse

Now you're here with your ruffled hair
And your blank stare brushes across the room
Brushing off my glare
Your boozy breath and your woozy step
You expose your neck,
So I can see the tender bruises left

Bruising my tenderness
That soft spot
That sponge that soaks up what I won't forget
I wonder if he'll always remember his hands on those hips
I wonder if you'll be with me when you think of it
Things I've never seen that I won't forget

I picture stolen love in the most wretched sense
Erotic-ness seems so treacherous
Such ugly feelings created by such a beautiful creation
Your love is a weapon that even has Eros shaken
Standing there looking like a blessing, cursing me
Looking like a lesson, deservingly
I'm stressing over the confession
Looking at how your legs stick
Seeing the remains of sins
Honey stains all below your hips
—The sweetest revenge

Guilty

Light twinkles in the shallow ponds
As they shimmer against your eyes
Stepping out of the shade to leave the darkness behind
Brightened light makes a crease in the corner
When you squint, it falls through the crease like a slide
Tears fall victim to this ground you worship
With your hands choking your thighs, choking on your cries
I barely look as I walk by
Nothing caught my eye
Beauty is in the eye of the beholder
I must be blind

You idolize imperfections
You unholy contamination
I'm even deceived by my deceitful offers
A heart leading me, only me to prosper
Searching for black gold in your living waters
Drilling it in, pushing deeper, harder
Malfunctioning drills alike
Polluting you from the inside
Death for the life you once sustained

Your stain
For my gain
I am willing to take this blame
What a shame, I'm so unashamed
Knowing you will let me explain

Now what is honesty without the option of dishonesty?
What is the offer of truth once exposed by the proof?
Facts—shunned off
In lieu of prideful character defenses
That can only incriminate
Because false judgements can only dissipate

If offense doesn't exist, it doesn't need defense
Fighting this closed case
Eyes rolling away from my plea
My own arm brings this gavel down on me

The security I breach
These alarms in tandem,
The renegade conscious of the thief
Darkness escaping from your light
Those shadows that follow
Bound and dragged along, like I am to the prison of emotion
Being called to account for your desecrated temple

Ghost of Love

My spirit screams
She's haunting my heart
From beyond my dreams
She tortures me awake
She taunts me in my sleep
I have fallen too deep

Poltergeist of my feelings
Keeps me from feeling;
By keeping these feelings
She's been keeping me feeling

I pull and she'll snatch
She pushes, I push back
Then she pushes me from the back
I don't see her coming
They don't see why I'm running
She appears and I'm jumping
They say I'm jumping at nothing

I have fallen so deep
Or she has fallen so deep
In me with her claws and her teeth
She shakes me and breaks me
She rips me and tears me apart
She's ruthless, I'm clueless; I ask why do you do this?

Her babble in rage
She shakes me; I'm rattled
On edge like on the edge of a battle
She's so angry, for what?
She snaps and I jump
From her whispers I run
She begs me to stay
But she pushes me away

With a stolen breath she blows me away
She makes me fall
And then wonders why I don't come when she calls
I ignore her to her face, but she's in my way
I tell her I love her, just wait
I say I'll be back, I lie to get by
She has no form of trust, she's so scorned
It's ok, I'm ok, though torn
Away
In my own world, where I buried her
Where she was never mourned

My world quakes
I curse her as I tremble
As my wall breaks
My words are so little to the words she leaves in my mental
Karma's sentence
A hardened heart against
A hearts vengeance
Why, Love? Why love?
Why does she go on; why does she not go on?
Restless spirit
She says I'm the reason she's dead and gone

Listen

I didn't hear the silence
Inside, I never saw the storm
Now the fallen rain blurs those flashing lights
So sick, my stomach tight
Trembling whispers of despair fill the air
I should've heard it, when I saw you last night

I wanted you that first night
I didn't know it would've been your first night
I remember how you would flirt like,
You just knew I was the worst type
You wanted something, and you didn't know why
I wanted something I saw deep in your eyes
I was searching for something I thought I'd never find
While you were trying to find something deep in your mind
I tried to probe your mind,
As I watched your body language yield signs
But you played your cards close
Even after I showed you all of mine
Your decisions declared war,
I saw your face drawing long battle lines
I knew then there was a struggle
But it wasn't mine
And you were taking too much time
And I didn't have the time

I wish I took the time
I wish I never left your side
I should've seen it in your sigh
I just couldn't see why you couldn't see the truth in me
You should've seen it in that guy
You let him take what you withheld from me
And you let him break what I would've held protectively

But you ran back to me
Expecting me to receive you affectionately
Like I'm supposed to wait on you until he's through
Taking me for a man that's weak
For you
I won't be a plan B
You should've chosen me
One look in those red eyes and I see
The truth that hurts
And something in me wants you to hurt like me

I care
But then I selfishly care for me
What you need, I ignore for the petty me
I can't hold you,
I have to hold my composure
In the closure of emotionally charged apologies
Wrapped up in myself, you leave,
That look warning me
Silently begging me
But so loud, this ego of mine

Signs misread
Things I said, caught up in my pride
I saw you try to hide your tears,
Acting like I didn't care why
I hid my feelings and I muted my cry
Blocking your view so you couldn't see that side

Only if I would've put myself aside, and been by your side
Only if I would've . . . why did I . . . ?
Damn . . .
Why did you . . . ?
All the if's and why's I have inside

No objection, I should have never been a judge
I know the pain of rejection,
I should have never withheld love

Only if I could've . . .

I know if you would've just . . .

Man . . . we both should've . . .

But since you didn't . . .

And since I didn't . . .

I will never know why
Why you wanted to die

UNINTENDED
the outcome of actions compelled without plans or thoughts of the end results

Never Learn

My cup is cold, the coffee hot
My fingers frozen to the spot
My heart is cold, so cold, so cold is not

My body shivers, triggers my arm to tremble
My coffee is strong and black, nothing sweet
My cup is filled to the rim
My weak arm outstretched
So the coffee doesn't get on me
But my feet are so far in front of me
My shoes are the victim, dark stains seeping into them

Dots and spots, easy to get off
I try to wipe them away, but I rub them in
And these dots and spots connect, my problems bigger
What a mess

Too nonchalant for it to be much stress
My heart is cold, I can't hear my feet
They scream to me, they start to feel the heat
But I don't feel it seep
And if so, I won't feel it deep
The heat doesn't warn, it doesn't even warm

I'm cold to the core
A frozen fort for my sores
Clogging my pores, locking my doors
Someday I may find a remedy
Someway
My shoes will be spotless eventually

I don't worry, though I hurry
I pick back up the pace, my footsteps become blurry
Another drop on my shoes won't concern me
My arm outstretched as I run,
I still hold my trembling cup
I wonder how else it can hurt me
…until it burns me

> This clown just never learns.
> Please don't be that idiot running around with a hot cup of coffee splashing on himself. What a damn fool. I wanna punch him.

And if he comes around me dropping hot coffee on me,
I am gonna punch him. I'm gonna punch him down!
Accident or not.
The fool needs to sit down somewhere
Then he needs to wipe off his dripping cup and drink his coffee first
And then he needs to wipe down those dirty shoes with those brown stains
Like it's alright
Like that's just cool
That shit ain't cool!
Talking about he don't care what I think
When I punch him, he's gonna care what I think
He's gonna be holding his face asking me, "Why did you do that?"
Talking about, "What did I do?"
And that's just gonna make me wanna punch him again
– Fool

Somebody or something will teach him a lesson if he won't learn on his own.
But trust me, no one wants to learn the hard way, and no one should.

Open your eyes
See the signs
Use the knowledge
Use your mind
Take heed!

5.

Dysfunction
#5496875   #54921821

Love should not confuse me
Love should not discourage me
Love should not defile me
Love should not hurt me
Love should not leave me empty . . .

Dysfunction happens when we let emotions rule. Like a leaf being blown by the wind, we react to events or to the will of others instead of taking the initiative. Such responses may be rooted in defense or desperation, but they rarely originate from our true desires. Therefore, we are no longer true to ourselves in reaction.

Strive to remain conscious of not only *how* you feel, but *why* you feel a certain way. Emotion is the indicator of our well-being and that of our situations. Evaluate your state of mind, and if negativity is present, consider a new direction. Focus on what you want, not on what you don't want. With a clear, desirable ideal in mind, concentrate on corresponding thoughts. Simply turning in the right direction mentally will bring about the inspiration necessary to progress and prosper. By following this inspiration, we can implement necessary changes—changes based on new ideals, not merely old reactions that have been tweaked.

Although we are doing a new thing, it will feel right. This is how we are meant to function. We are to keep our emotions in check. Our mind should never be led by emotions. Emotions are to follow our thoughts, by order and by submission. Therefore, we must keep our thoughts in check. Then, being led by the intent of healthy desires, our wants will become our haves.

This is how we break the cycle of dysfunction.

Cold Heart

How can you see me and not see me,
When I always see you and you're not here
How can you hear me and not hear me,
When I hear me without speaking
How can you touch me and not feel me
How can I feel so much, and not be felt

On fire for you
This ice on me
I burn in this passion
Waiting for hail to melt
As flames turn to embers
This bright light moving
Into this dim glow
Now these warm coals only cast shadows
Cooling

Running into this freezing wind
Unprepared for this weather
Exposed limbs
Expecting a summer swim
A frozen lake
Broken through as I hop in
To a drowning heart
Kept on ice
Preservation

So many bodies in this frozen grave
Dead lives
We aren't meant to save
I came to get you
I couldn't reach you

I thought I jumped in after you
But I really fell
As they now fall for me
As they reach for me
As they freeze for me
—Another heart going cold

Rebound

You ease the pain
But I still feel the pain
When you break my tough skin
Easing your sweet needle in
As you mend my heart
By sowing your seeds
In a bed full of weeds
You try to take a place that's been taken
But forsaken
In a space I wish you could find
I'm so lost in between the lines
In meanings
Or still not believing

Persuade me
Find a place to take me
Find a place they couldn't take
Some things you can't replace
I need you to tell me I don't need to
I need you to show me something
I can't see through
To see why I need to
I need you
I just need something to numb me
But I'm still feeling something

This pleasant distraction
A new attraction
To make love
To create love
To not know I fake love
Until you're not there
Until you're both there
When I'm aware I compare
When there's something in the air
Emotional affair
Mentally I'm still there

Even though I decide to go in a new direction
I'm still tripping over the following steps
Still falling in the void that was left
Open, so you seem to fit
Open to your love
Only because of the closure I can never get

Covers

Crazy bitch, crazy bitch
Operation make me sick
Crazy bitch, crazy bitch
Occupation demolition

Stay away from this building
It was broken down, I tried to fix it
You destroy it every time I try to build it
That's why I fired you
But you still bring your wrecking ball into my business
Breaking up a new foundation with it
Running my new partner off
Tearing apart my life

Like a broken heart was not enough
Like my pain is never enough
What do you gain?
Whatever it is it's never enough

Crazy bitch, you do too much
Crazy bitch, crazy bitch
I would never have guessed it

You look so good,
The inside was never questioned
This is not one of those "but I'm grateful for it" lessons
Poisonous berry

Book covers, a lovely color
Muting every other
Shade,
Shady
Bad Judgment

I admit I liked the cover
So I bought a whole subscription
Possession, greed
Why the hell did I get it?!
Enticement, tempting
Now I say I don't want it
They still send it

Then one day I wonder when it finally went away
That's the day I start to miss it
And that's the day I finally get it
I see the cover, the best one since
Maybe it's better now
Once again it piques my interest
I open it . . .
. . . And it's the same old shit

Abusive

Why am I here
After drying all those tears
After you turned your back
Shrugging your shoulders as mine went slack
Why am I back
Thinking back . . .

Why did I call back?

I told myself I was tired of hearing the rings of missed calls
Chimes from "sorry" messages
I know I should delete
Curiosity?
Or do I just want to hear you speak?
Feigning annoyance, crossed arms
What could you possibly have to say?
The spawn of the argument
I have to respond

The last word
Desperate victory
Leave me, but leave me with my dignity
The need to be understood
The need for understanding
On my terms
I finally get to
Closure
Getting too close

Your opening
My excuse
You drug me back
All these things you drag me through . . .
I call it drug abuse
I just need another dose
Over and over
And then it's an overdose

Spiteful

My heart says I fell in love
My mind thinks I fell in a trap
Those soft hands caressing my hair,
Holding my head in her lap

My hands ease up her tee
Her hands ease me away, as I reach that upper sleeve
Maybe she's shy
Or maybe she's just cautious
Maybe in time she'll let me see
I figure it's love
How it seems like a need
But only to even a score
Even though I wasn't even on board

Casualties of war, innocent victims
Revenge on exes
Battle of the sexes
Telling her friends how she simply won
Like how friends gather and laugh at fools
Because it's simply fun
Underlying intentions of those beautiful smiles
Pretty girls, ironic perceptions
Like pretty guns

Venus guy trap, deadly flowers
Thorns in my flesh from the rose bush
Once the lightning bug in my soul looks
And I can't help myself
Like when that grudge gives her that nudge

Clandestine lover,
Those weapons hidden underneath her trench coat
Uninvited invites
Tones that disarm all alarms, opening that door with a gasp
Throwing me off like boomerangs, and her aim is true
Misdirection

I've let my guard down leading her past each defense
Now I see I'm a hostage, I see her true form
Her mask melts
I mourn
That death grip
Holding my heart in contempt
Because hell hath no fury like a woman scorned

Snake

Loyalty
Your forgery
I see the signs
Crooked letters beginning my name where you signed
Your slithering untraced
So wrapped up in your embrace
The target for your darting tongue
Piercing words that always won
Keep it one hundred, in my eye
Until you shed your disguise

Because it's all bull!
Corny jokes and calculated laughs
Suspicious eyes
Suspecting suspecting
Little lies filling a king bed
Little lies in flower beds
Big weeds, those bad seeds

The fruit of my harvest
You worm your way in
A mouth that ruins
Your words
Pollutants
Chemically imbalanced
Emotionally ravaged
The drug that makes me feel well
As it kills cells

Undercover, hateful lover
The ugly moles of pretty faces
So many faces
That I begin to favor
Until I'm looking in the mirror
Seeing between the lines
To see I'm divided
Losing half

Scissors

To cut you off, I'd probably cut myself in the decision
It will leave a scar
Even if it's done with precise precision
And to remove the scar would require another incision
And yet another mark, marked from being apart

You said you could stand the rain
Then came a hurricane, what happened to your levy?
You said you would hold steady, but you were never ready
Now get ready, hold steady, I'm swinging this machete!

You said I was too much of a player
But the jersey was easy for me to take off
Then you saw those ballers
And all of a sudden you want to play ball
Now I don't want to hear your yelling or screaming
When you see my Texas Chainsaw!

Your friends are always fishing
And they reel in the right!
They try to catch me in a lie
Their opinions are pursuits
But with you I ride, or die
The things they say is all you see
Things they don't even see!
Why don't you rely on facts?
Like we are Siamese – I got your back
When I try to move forward, you bring us back
Ok, I'll be back,
With my axe!

It wasn't smart to rock the boat
Now all we do is go back and forth
What a relation-ship! I want to throw you overboard
I would, if it wasn't for this cord
I'm so glad I have this sword!

But our ties have been worn so thin
All I'll probably need is some scissors

The loss of your sweetness makes me so bitter
Becoming my own killer
Slowly going for the heart

Then I came to, relieved
They were just scissors

DYSFUNCTION
the perfect design of a person or persons being misused—their specific purpose not being fulfilled

Stage Left

I'm seeing clearer
I'm seeing through the smoke I've subconsciously created
I see the big picture for what it really is
And not just what my faith in you pics apart from it
I'm stepping out of the picture and letting the reel roll on…
Without me
I am a man who takes the necessary exit
I'm not to be where I'm not wanted
I don't need the throne
The throne needs me
Lovers and friends, a love with a friend
But, I guess these times have gone by like time has gone by
I'm not of importance like other things governing your life
I don't mind the backseat
But there is no backseat in the two-seater
Reality speaks . . . as actions speak . . .
Loud!
And I have two ears
Like I have two fingers
—Deuces

P.S. I honestly thought this love would never run out . . .
I just hope you feel it was worth it . . .
Juicing me of every drop
Sincerely,
Your never-again

Exits are entrances to new dimensions of life. Where there is the will to sacrifice, lying underneath in motive, there will be desire unmet.

Beyond where there is desire, if you so dare to strive, over the bridges reaching from lack . . . there will be found fulfillment.

6.

Worth
#7495947 #74921021

No longer will I venture down your one-way street
The way you never come
The way I, only I, must always go
This merry-go-round you run beside
But leave me spinning on my own
I open my dizzy eyes reaching out for support,
Falling
Then I see I'm alone
Slowly I rise to awareness
It hurt, but I'm not hurt
Pain reminds me to protect myself
I'm too valuable to get hurt
And you don't even pay attention,
But I know what I'm worth

So I know you are not worth it

Separating ourselves from someone or something we are attached to is not easy. It takes strength and discipline to fight these urges and desires. It is a pain in the brain, but a pain the brain is designed to endure in order to elevate in desire and faith. Pain summons strength that will otherwise remain dormant. This growth brings wisdom that validates our choices, ensuring that our desires will be healthy and appropriate for us.

In the aftermath, we can recognize our worth. And we can discern who or what is worth our attention and time. Time is the most valuable asset we can give in life; we can never get time back. We are spending time when we are paying attention. Some people or things aren't worth that price. A waste of time is even worse than a waste of money; we can get money back. We should never invest ourselves when we are not seeing a return. There is so much more we can enjoy, build, and accomplish with our precious energy. The right people and things increase, cultivate, and make the most of this energy. We must see past the surface and superficialities in order to make a solid evaluation of our subjects of interest. This includes seeing beyond the surface to recognize worth in others also. We must remain aware that desire and denial can blind us. It's like being tempted to buy my favorite car as a primary mode of transportation, but its engine is missing and cannot be replaced; no matter how much I love it, it is a foolish investment.

Crush

I hope you notice
That I notice
I hope you notice
That you are my focus
That I am so focused
And I also noticed
You don't have to be a poet
To make poetry
As I read unspeakable things
That take a hold of me
Finding myself in an aura so intriguing
So lost in the meaning

I find myself seeing
I find myself looking
A little too much
And a little too long
As you sing along
I know every song
I know every phrase
All the little things that you say
I know all the ways to make you smile
So I've mastered all the ways
I know what every look means,
The same with every tone
I know when it's something else,
No matter how you make it seem

I know what you would say
I know what you would think
And as I watch you think, I know what you will say
I know every order, I know how to make your drink
I know your favorite color, your favorite place to eat
I understand the façade on the surface
Because I know what's hidden in the deep

I always try to make it right
Before they even notice something's wrong
I know what makes you strong
I know what makes you weak
I know what cheers you up
I know what gets you back up after a round of defeat
I know just what you need to hear
I know what makes you win
Because I know what makes you a winner

I noticed when you shivered
Gave up my coat in the winter
I notice before you start to sweat
And I fetch the ice in the summer
I noticed you'd be a good mother
And I noticed the way you look at babies
Even though you say you never want them

When she crossed you I noticed, when he hurt you I noticed
When you needed to talk I noticed
It's hard for me to talk when I try to explain why I notice
So I just show it
Hoping you notice
But it just goes unnoticed

And I finally notice
But still, I think about it so much
From your vibe to your touch
Anticipating love with all my love
But my hopes are not enough
I stood on that hope for so long
And now it's finally crushed!

Her Pool

I'm not intimidated by her
But I fear her
What I will do to be near her
No control, my remote controller
Every time I push up
My strength soaker
Cardio, with her
Over and over
Everything I can give, I am willing to put out
It doesn't matter how much work I put in
Just as long as we can work out

She doesn't know which buttons to push
She thinks below the words in my looks
My thoughts go over her head
She doesn't pay attention
To things I'll never mention
Body language betraying me
But it's okay, she never listens
She brightens up my life
But she can't see my soul glisten
Other valuables in sight
Jewels of earthly might

So as I hold her tight, I hold my lips tight
With all my might, although
I can't stop my spirit as it flows
Into her soul
Then all of a sudden I'm turned off
And I have to pull away
I have to let go
Because there's nowhere else for it to go
—She's too shallow

Selfish Gifts

You open up, but never open up
You let me in, but never let me in
You know I love you, but it works for you
That leash that you love to pull
Your toy without the batteries
Or batteries of flattery
You come to me to be satisfied
Then let me down and toss me aside

The feeling makes me weak, the feeling's too strong
You let me kiss you long
You let me fill my palms
You let me feel you up
You let me touch you there
You let me go all the way
But in reality I'm going nowhere

How you sit there
Under my stare
Impatient eyes beckoning, devilishly
From behind your disheveled hair
Your hair down
Like my guard goes
Like those swallows
As your dress follows

Then you use me for your soothing
The antidote for the abusing, that you're abusing
Your prescriptions, you come to get filled
Fulfill your addiction
I'm the bond for your mission
Then you leave me with this feeling

This is all you're here for
That sex with those filters
Keeping love out of the way

You get yours, then prepare your getaway
Those thoughts once you can think
Those expressions that block my words to conversate
Interruptions or excuses, it all means the same
For all those other same things
I can never get you to stay
Not even on the phone
You call, only one thing you want
I always tell you what I want, you always tell me don't…start…
What can I do for all I want?
Except accept a part
What we share, all these shares
But I see I'm investing too much, this bank can easily break
Making deposits in your vault
But you won't keep my heart safe

Unfair Exchange

I hold my heart close
Because this is my life
I harden it to protect it
What would I do if it was hurt?
I'd hurt worse
What would I do if he was killed?
I'd die

If I open up my heart for you, what would you see?
The scars, the stitches, the wounds, and how it bleeds
The ugly, the nasty, would you look at it in disgust
You'd look at the damage, and be unsure if it's sure,
Not sure if it's something you'd trust
Or would you look and see how it survived through that much
It's been broken and discarded
Abandoned and stolen

I used to wear it on my sleeve
It was put to the test
A hardened heart lured it
It was torn like the rest
In the pain there was gain
When muscles tear they will heal and become stronger
But it stayed inside my chest, like its bulletproof vest
To reject effects
Still no proof
The reject effect
No desire but to desire, no quest to connect
Lest it infects
And it won't confess, I confess
What you suggest must be jest

Why should I give you my heart?
For you to operate your ploy
Why should I give you my heart?
So you can open it up, and play with it like a toy?
Why should I give you my heart?
That's not what it's for
Why should I give you my heart?
When you won't give me yours

Losing What I Never Had

I opened up my world to a closed door
And a cleaned house
I wonder what you sold me for
I thought I fell in love
I just fell in my dream

Face first, I hit my head
So is the pain just all in my head?
I swore, I fell for you
I fell for the prank, I think
Assumptions that he made
My mind playing tricks
He seems to love his little games

I fell on my face
The image fell upon the mirror
Now a spider web beholds me
Now I barely know me
I got to hold it together
Because you're not here to hold me
You led me on, a little bit
I was the pony
The truth hurts
I liked it better when it was phony

I cry over your lies
But I'd rather lie beneath your lies,
Than to lie here and hear my cries
Cover the truth as we lie beneath your comforter
Only you can console me
Emotion's remote
Even if you must control me, please change what's showing
Where is your costume, your clothing?
I can't hang it up, though it's unfolding
Things we will do when we're lonely

Things I should've seen you never showed me
Things I saw only because I looked too far
Mirages, I mourned over every one as I lost it
Experiences for precautions
Lessen my losses
Because there are only lessons, not losses

WORTH

the definite quality and importance of someone holding a particular value deserving of something of a certain standard

7.

Growth
#9487267 #94859687

I have let this pain build up inside of me
To the point it has become a part of me
It would cost too much to tear it down
I'm past the point of starting over
Instead I transform
This stumbling block into a foundation
An application
Now that I have the power
To see how my losses serve as lessons
Now that I have the power
To see how my perseverance is my strength
To Grow

Pain is Gain

Negative events, situations, circumstances, and relationships can be destructive. As physical pain occurs in the physical self, spiritual pain indicates a negative effect on the spirit. But the pain can be helpful as a suggestion, even a warning. It may be that you are not going in the right direction, not being fulfilled, or endangering yourself or your destiny.

Growth begins when we shift from blaming pain on bad luck or others' faults and begin looking within for the answer, for the cause. We make the choices that lead us to the painful places. It is not by chance, unless you leave it to chance. You make the decision between investing wisely or rolling the dice.

With the understanding that our pain is a product of our choices—and that our choices stem from our thoughts—we have the power to reverse the pain by reversing thought. We have the power to heal ourselves. In this truth, we gain constructive wisdom that helps shape our character.

We must acknowledge defective causes within us. Only then can we choose a different cause, the right cause, to formulate the right effect. Experience can build us up to defend our minds against negatives, preparing us to defeat future obstacles.

Take advantage of every disadvantage. This is perseverance. Build faith, aspire hope, reserve power. We must embrace this power and realize this power is always

—Growing

Misery

Misery, misery
Come to me misery
Misery, misery
You have been missing me
Misery, misery
How did you get to me?
I'm so sick of you misery,
But not as much as I'm sick of me
Misery, misery
I am so into you
Misery, misery
You talk and you listen too
Misery, misery
I will come live with you

Misery,
We cannot be together
I try not to notice
You are my focus, when I'm so out of focus
My heart is so swollen, my flesh is so soaken
The words you have chosen
For the words I have spoken
I am so broken
Broken from consoling

My need that you need me
Their needs, why they need me
They will deceive me
They won't believe me
Please me, my misery
Better off not alone
Please do not free me
Misery! Misery!
Please don't leave me
As they leave me
In you
My misery

My Ways

How can you expect me to tell you yes,
When all I've ever heard was no?
All I've ever known was rejection
I don't know an exception, how do I make an exception?
How can I accept you?
I don't know acceptance
All I know is no!
How do I know where to go?
And how do I allow you to go where I'm not allowed?
Can you receive allowance from a man with no money?

No!
All I ever heard was no
What other way would I know?
I had to make my own way
But you wouldn't accept my way
It's not accepted
And how would I make a way for you if you don't know my way?
Even if there was a way, I would say no way
No way, it's that way; that way is no way
There's no way

This is how I get along, because I could never get along
How could I take you along?
Why would I take you along?
So you could say what you would say – "no" to my way
No way!

Ways that stuck with me along the way
Stuck, so I stay
Stuck in my ways

Dwelling

Sitting on the edge of the tide
To decide
To accept to be denied
As the waves kiss the earth
As the light stretches out, and the sun hugs the sky
And I look up at the clouds, looking for an answer
But when the wind whispers against my face
I don't know how to answer

I consider a response of this nature, I almost understand
I attempt to grasp what's fleeting
Stressed fingers I dig into the sand, it sticks to my hand
I am unable to isolate a single grain
I wish I could blend in as it can
If I disappear I won't be here
And close enough to hear

I'm burning inside
The fire licks my soul
Then its tongue enters my heart,
I come to finish my thoughts
Although I don't know where they start
That's when I lose myself again
Where does it end?
I try to hold on to the times, but the time I just spend
I try to find change for my mind, but I just get paper again
What I don't wish to save, I give away with the flick of a pen
To my dismay, it stays
And it will never end

Like the world never ends, although they say it's ending
Like the losers think they're winning
Well, it is the finish line, they're just stuck at their beginning
I pity the fish that can't stop swimming
I'm drowning in thoughts
But my mind seems to never perish

I choke to death, but stay alive
A strangled immortal, my face a permanent purple
How am I feeling boxed-in
By this permanent circle?

Hurdle after hurdle
And when I fall, I look up
It looks like a wall
And it gets higher and higher the longer I stall
Time and time again, it's like it's time again
If my mind will only stop, something only time will end
I think until then
No
Wait
I know
It will be killing me slow

Missing My Flight

Reaching for the sky
My hands held high
Reaching for the sky with my hands
As my feet sink quickly in quicksand

Reaching for the sky as the birds fly by
I wonder, where could I get some wings?
I wonder how it feels to be the leaves
Swaying in the maple
All I feel is the serpent as he tightens around my ankles

I reach for the sky
Finally able to bring my feet high
But it only makes me mad
As soon as I come up, I come back

Why am I ashamed of these things?
Ashamed of these arms that aren't wings
You birds who I admire, I know you must get tired
Can you not fly higher?
Why do I drag my legs in defeat?
Why, because they're not as tall as trees?
You leaves are way up there, but you are going nowhere
Why should I be you, when I should exceed you?
My eyes just complain to my brain, making it insane
Why would I try to fly, when I have a plane?

Chasing the Runner

Listening to their approval
Ignoring myself
Loving this world
More than I love myself
Those who stay true to the game
But lie to their wife
Double life

They see a part of me
I can never show my mom
The boy she loved is gone
He died in my arms
I left him in the streets
They accept it was the streets
No one sees it was me
I run to be free
Like runaways running to child slavery
Then I look into the mirror and I can't see me
Or I can't see how it can be
When I can't tell which me is me

I left the path
I was swallowed up by the tall grass
When I forget who the real me is
Lost in what I become in the streets I run
The lies we live
Finding myself dying to self is
The breath I lose
Running from the truth

Though I don't know where I'm going
For reasons I don't know, he knows my path
This stranger reminds me of my past
But I don't think he can recognize me in this mask
I hurdle without slowing, leaping over every obstacle in my path
I'm gaining at last, but my lead doesn't last

He hops all the hurdles and gains on me fast!
I turn, he runs past; I tricked him at last!
Then I feel breath on my back, I look back,
He's not that far back!
I even lose myself, still I don't lose him

Wherever I run he catches up quick!
What have I done? He runs and won't quit!
What do I have that he's so determined to get?!

I run through the storm as the thunder throws fits
I'm heavy from rain, and I can see that he's drenched
I run through the desert, my thirst makes me sick
He doesn't stop to be quenched

I run through the night, through darkness without light
How am I still in his sight?!
I run with all my might
But I'm so tired, that I'm even tired of fright
I'm tired of trying so hard
In this race I won't win
To be in a place for no trophy
There's no finish line, there's no end
As I slow down he gets closer
I finally get to take him in
But I can't believe that it's him…

It's me chasing me!
Why am I running from him?

The Climb

I slip
I try to catch myself
I struggle to get a grip
In the midst of moving mountains
That hover over valleys
I'm knocked down in
Despair

This place I've found myself in
I'd rather any other place
It doesn't matter where
In desperation I lose myself
To settle
Though I was given a gift
To pilot mountains
Invisible flair
Reservations for cockpits upon peaks
But I can't seem to get there
I can't see a way to get there

The mountains are so high, heights hidden by the sky
I don't know where they go, for the sky I don't know
This valley is so low
Even when the sky is clear
My eyes do not show what I wish to know
The valley is too low

My path is rough, my feet filled with cuts
The rocks are so jagged, and I'm scratched by the shrubs
As I walk I look up
I walk and look up
I look up at the great walls
If I climb I may fall

But around every bend, I see there is no end
I walk and I walk, I walk and I walk
I walk until I'm no longer walking at all
I climb and I fall, I climb and I fall, I climb and I fall
Until I see no point in climbing at all
So I just walk, I just continue to walk
Until I see no point in walking at all

So I climb and I fall, I climb and I fall, I climb and I fall
Until there is nothing better than climbing to fall
So I climb and I fall, and I climb and I fall, and I climb
Until I'm no longer climbing at all
I reach and I grab, I reach and I grab, and I reach
Until there's nothing else to grab
I'm reaching for the sky, as I open my eyes

What a surprise! What do I know?
I look down below
Where did it go?
Oh,
The valley's too low

Weakness

The reason, or the excuse
The wrongful use, abuse
Nothing I should turn from, but to learn from
I see it as to hold me back, but it's to force me to push forward
To grow, to improve, to build
Stumbling blocks that train us to be surefooted
That room for improvement; renovation
Building character, who we are, who we want to be
Turning what we see into what we want to see

Who are we without challenges?
Who do we become once they come?
Trophies for the underdog,
Like a kingdom usurped by the oppressed

Never to define me, but to refine me
Never to mistake a door for a boundary
Without those walls closing in on me erected,
I wouldn't be subjected
To learn the strength, to rise
Above this "so-called" weakness

Better

Once I was broken, now I'm not
Tossed as a loss,
Now I've got what was lost
Forgotten
For me to have gotten this
Got to get nothing for all I have
I have enough to get enough

Once I was broken, I saw no need to be fixed
Fixing on a broken wish
Wishing wishes were legit
Like those wishing wishes which don't exist
You must not wish for what exists
For what you forget you must get for
Dream when you're asleep
When you're aware when it's there,
You must not look anywhere
If you are not there, it's getting there
That gets you there
Don't dream so deep you're still asleep when it's at your feet
When you sleep walk and walk past
To go back past what's in your past
So your dreams play dreams of your past
Wishing that your dream was cast
But dreams don't last

Awaken from what has been forsaken . . .
What is fixed?
Can you still break?
Do you recreate, or do you just use tape?
Was it meant to bear the weight,
Or was it meant to look in place?

What can you take?
Or what can you fake?
When shook up, what can you shake?
Made to fake?
You can't fake the real, really; it can really break
Made to last, made to make it
Make it last, make it great!

GROWTH
the cultivation of a being from a lower form of existence into a higher or more mature state

To See Destiny

These earthquakes that shake life
And break up concrete foundations
Of the route I choose to take
The cue for the directions through
These detours that force me to change my ways
Although my destination remains the same
Although I see this destination's the same
I see it in another way

Deeper than the surface
This urge to dive into the depths
I no longer crave to surf it
Bypass those waves that push me back
I need to be pulled beyond the current
Pulled into the mysteries
Enduring those pressures
That push upon my outer shell to birth pearls

> Destiny, you must seek
> Directions are unique
> Throughout these one-way streets
> Adorned with spectacular signs
> That make subtle peeks through this fog
> That sadly we seem to set our focus upon
> You must seek your life's purpose to find your way in life

THE PRESCRIPTION

8.

The Monster

#2895621 #28927315

My other face dwells underneath my cover
In starving darkness
Sleeping with one eye open
Seemingly unaware
All the while taking it all in
As I take in the pain
As I struggle with the hurt
As I fail to staunch the wound
It overflows
This is the fullness of my capacity
Overwhelmed
In absence of options
The other me takes over

At times, we have probably all related to Bruce Banner, the soft-spoken comic book scientist whose alter ego is the uncontrollable green rage machine, the Hulk. The monster was passed down from Bruce's father, though in real life, we often create our own monsters. Like the fictional character, our normally-dormant monster can explode in extreme reaction to overwhelming feelings or circumstances. Left drained and defeated, regretful and ashamed, we attempt to gain composure while we wonder, "What just happened? What did I do? Why did I do it?"

Bruce discovers that the Hulk only rises out of negativity and stress, so he learns to control his monster by controlling his mind. He understands that his thoughts affect his emotions, which influence his actions. He also understands that the situations he puts himself in affect his thoughts. Certain situations can cause unintentional reactions, which can lead to unintentional circumstances. Because Bruce's monster springs from anger and frustration, he learns the root causes that lead him to feel angry and frustrated. He relies on a new cause—peace and calm—to direct a new effect. Bruce waited too long to deal with the root cause to stop the birth of his monster, so he only has one option, to find a way To Tame the Monster.

Malice

This chalice forced upon me
In this sitting limbo
Soaking underneath this stained towel
What they heave to me they cannot bear
As I spew specks of foul
They dread to wear
This torture I can't pry away from
This gouging of my eye

An eye for an eye

I was wronged
That doesn't mean I wasn't wrong
Poking at tigers in cages
Then they blame the tiger
When he claws at their faces

A beast
Made for the jungle
He roams
When he no longer fits in the funnel
Called humble
Broken time glass

When it doesn't last
What a man can't stand
When he's told he can't stand
Pushed back
Held back
So he can't push back
When he's looked at
Like he isn't supposed to look back

His patience in pain
Against this wall
His patience in vain
Back against the wall
This fire he tries to maintain
Playing with fire they think they can tame
This fire he cannot contain
When they fan the flames
And everything goes up in flames

When that deafening roar escapes
When the one you think is under your control
Can't control
The uncontrollable
—Nature

Losing It

Born in pain
This ugly thing
Drinking my tears
Eating my fears
Consumed in the darkness I face
Consuming
Inhaling their hate
Exhaling …

In this intoxicated state
I stumble upon commands
Backed by a heavy hand
Backhanded
Remarks from this affliction I start
Cursing enemies
In the attacks I lead
On the war on me

. . . Empty threats
This threat of emptiness
The void where renegades gather
The absence of love
The Hate U Give
A T.H.U.G.

You who whisper by tongue,
And scream through looks
The self-acclaimed
I despise such righteousness
Unacceptable
We exiled kings bound by shadows of caves
Beneath mountains of darkness
Never welcomed into the light

My heart is right,
But it's not right about this fight
At war with love
How to bring peace to the unloved?
... This impossibility
Frustration building me
To topple their serenity
How would I know these subjects are in rebellion?
I end up against a higher power
Unknowingly

I only know God as a word in a book
The only rod I know has a barrel and a trigger
I put trust in a killing machine to save my life
I find comfort because they call me their nigga
In ignorance I willingly gave my life
We're owned by an abusive master
Hired shepherds take flight from the wolf at night
If I look back I'll only see the back of the pastor
Those who condemn with their eyes closed
They don't see how it will come down on their head
Mislead by what was mis-said
I worked to pay back what I never owed
I gave up on love
I missed the point of what was never told
I turned down the mint for counterfeit
From he who I was saved I gave my soul

Ulterior

Insurance for accidents
But we'll never know if it's their purpose
Friends are liabilities
Trust is my enemy
Like officers in plain clothes
Infiltrating my inner circle
Multi-tasking ice picks, first breaking ice
Opening up to the Trojan horse

War is a constant
An intention or in tension
The potential of a stalker
To be pushed, to be provoked
We walk along that thin ice, we're cool
For now,
The abyss is just frosted over

Poisonous ingredients
Food fights
Battles at my dining table
Leaving a bad taste in my mouth
I'll die before I figure it out

A cancer
Taking me, a part
A part of me, apart from me
Me against me
Mine against me
Mind against me
An enemy I feed
As he influences my truest
As he closes out my closest
As he weakens my strongest
All his lies are honest

An opponent I never met
Though we always meet
An opponent I train
An opponent on my team
Opposing allies, invisible enemies

My throat slit from behind
From behind the bulletproof glass in my armored truck
I never saw it coming
Bombs in my secret hideout
The one no one knows about
Aiming at the enemy
My trusty gun backfires
Displaced enemies
The Judas Iscariot of my empire
I try to figure out why, I'm at a loss
I'm blown away as he talks
His confession is a chilling wind from this cross

Checks

Breach of respect
You reject common ground
Pride we protect

Residential battleground
No politics, no president
You declare war on my soul
You never know what it can take
Or what it can hold
Or what will happen once it unfolds
Or once it explodes

No more talks, I'm out of breath
It's been a long walk, now I'm out of steps
Just as the Messiah fulfills his word
I must quench this nerve
This twitch, this itch
No more meds that never do what they said
They just put a cloud in my head
This cloud over my life
This darkness
I seek shelter in life
Looking for light

But I only see red
You spilled blood in our bed
You'll lie in it
These wounds you open and won't allow to heal
Numbing me
This pain you claim I'm not allowed to feel
Becoming me
This pain
You will feel because it's what you steal

Guilty, before you even step a foot in my court
Guilty for not even stepping a foot in my court
How can we get even?
You never report, only by retort
How will we get even?
How I hate you make me resort out of hate
This sport of war
Fair to ask you to open your door
But now it must be opened by force

Forced on such a course
To address you at last
Checks that never bring cash
Checks that only cost
Who said love don't cost a thing?
—Now look at all I've lost

Retaliation

All you see . . .
Red . . .

You can no longer see
Loved ones who leave
In emergency
Heartbeat
Frantic
Late night phones speak
Silent responses
Legs going weak
Can't breathe
Still rushing back to your feet

Breathe
Unsteady breaths
Having to tell yourself to breathe
Unsure steps
Dreading what's already known
Still having this hopeless hope
Like it's still unknown

Sparks from a barrel muting life as it relays
That final deafening report it offers
Lift your fallen face for the report of the doctor
Don't want to look, but have to see
Next of kin, hate this honor
Can't wait to turn this hate into honor
In honor
Fallen waters like rivers of lava
Burn as you feel the accord of the monster

That burn that burns down security of walls
Surrounding your beast who sleeps through peace
Straining his chain
Inner screams that cannot be contained,

You have to let them out; you must release
Disturbances in the links
You struggle to keep it all together
Until it all breaks down
Until it's been unleashed

You may tremble from the tremors in hate's wake
But for love's sake
Beware when the indestructible intends destruction
Mushroom-clouded minds
Exploding brains
Cannot be contained
Atomic rage
Feel this shockwave

Tears and curses, death for life
Postmortem promises
Made to victims
To make victims
On their knees
Praying to karma
Getting answers out of guns

Searching the darkness for light
Logic expunged
Down at the lowest
Feel life plunge

Black rush
High strung
No fix without funds
They'll pay with their life
Like taking them will take it back
The debt still unsettled
Still will settle
For something like that
Knowing on this earth there's nothing exact
Just wanting them back

Why, God? Fighting God
But there's no fighting God
Inhale death at hand
But this drug wears off
It's back to this struggle
How Satan handles a perfect picture
Looking at life, it's now a puzzle
The thief takes one piece
To take peace apart

One bite from the serpent
And the poison corrupts the heart
When wars start
Revenge,
—Where war never ends

Suicide Note

Read these signs
Rejection, neglection
See, I was never worthy
So, who can tell me that it's not worth it
You can no longer hear these cries
I'm in the howling wind
My heart was knocked off my sleeve
It was broken, so I left it
On the mountain that was moving

I jumped off a cliff
Someone lied,
Someone said it was a porch
I may have died
I never realized
Thrown off by pride
Caught in the crossfire

I stepped into a warzone
I thought it was a street
I saw a man die
They called it a loss
Now I'm scared of defeat
Murder men, then call it victory

Manipulate men and call it a win
It seems like every time I win
I end up losing a friend
Every time I find a friend
He's just trying to win
This circle of friends
I wonder why I'm in
This cycle I never try to end

Somehow I still feel love amongst the heartless
Embraced by thugs
How do I feel so secure
When my house is full of thieves?
The self-righteous starve me
I lost my appetite for morals
My table adorned with stolen dinners
Nothing to lose

Nothing to keep safe
That's not in the safe
Like light, life, faith
Why do I feel so safe
When I'm surrounded by killers?

Kept behind codes
Speaking what's unheard
Hearing what's silent
Basking in the darkness
But how do I feel so alive
When I'm surrounded by death?

I know why . . .

I've already died
—I gave this monster my life

My Monster

The monster, he's here some nights
He's here some days, hidden in plain sight
Why am I the only one who sees him,
Why am I his only victim?
He only comes when I have no help
Maybe because I have no help
And when I call for help, it never helps
They don't believe me
They never believe me
In my bedroom, where I'm never sleeping, where I sleep
I never make a peep
Hiding underneath the sheets
Acting as if I'm asleep
But it doesn't stop him from getting to me
In the bathroom, where I let down my guard
In tears
He comes at me hard
I fight, but I'm too weak
The more I fight, the worse it will be

Night after night
If I don't see him, nightmares bring the sight
Day after day
My world's wasting away as he plays
I'd rather die this time, than to let him take me alive

But before I take my life, before I write the note
As I cry alone, someone tells me this is not the way to go,
He tells me I will never gain control,
Without a monster of my own
My Monster

As I grow, he grows with my every worry
The support for my every weakness
But his strength becomes another weakness

This monster is mine, but a monster alike
I watch him defend me
I watch them fight
But in the realm of monsters there are endless fights
Endless battles
So now I'm fighting three
While fighting to control the one that fights for me
Monsters have no loyalties; monster free-for-all
My enemy defeats my enemies
Then without more to do, my monster leaves, eventually
But I can't separate the feelings of grief and relief
As I look over my ruined city

MONSTER
a person with a malicious manner driven by a cruel nature, defying all morality and principle

9.

To Tame the Monster

#9875624 #98712417

Releasing this pain into the world
Anger, rage, malice
Expressions of a heart
Darkened by the world's effects
Releasing this pain
Only brings more pain
The cycle only becomes more painful
This inner war tires my soul
My spirit aches for peace
There must be a way

To tame the monster

Satan is the most extreme example of a monster. His insidious pride became arrogance, and "he fell like lightning from heaven," defeating himself. Even so, the fool continues waging a war he can never win.

Not all monsters are as obvious. There are the egotistical, the ambitious, the conniving. And not all monsters originate in anger and frustration; some are conceived by fear, ignorance, manipulation, mistreatment, insecurity, and neglect. All these thoughts, feelings, and ideas manifest in negativity, another form of evil. Evil develops when inner conflict collaborates with outer conflict, however subtle it may seem. Sometimes love is deemed as unworthy, so it finds its place in hate. Sometimes passion cannot be expressed, so frustration grows. Sometimes expectations are not met, and resentment develops.

These developments become our personal monsters, unconsciously formed to battle the pain, to fend off the attack of unchecked negative consciousness. They can grow until they're no longer controllable. And when they have nothing else to defeat or destroy, their hunger will turn inward and devour us from the inside out.

Therefore, we must find peaceful ways to release or risk exploding. When you feel yourself becoming mad, sad, frustrated, or depressed, fight back. This is a fight. When your fuse is short or your tank is empty, don't let resistance push you around. Push back. You have the power to just shove it out of the way. It may come back, but keep fighting. Find a way: working out, running, singing, dancing, writing, painting, or meditating. Find something you enjoy, something that brings you peace. The goal is to channel this negative energy into a productive and/or constructive expression.

It takes time and unprecedented patience for us to gradually form these new habits. Exercising these new ways to release this negative energy in an unharmful way strengthens our new causes to eventually resolve our dysfunction and dissolve the related undesirable effects. We must remain conscious of our thoughts, feelings, situations, and surroundings. The thinker is the master. We must tame the monsters that we create, ultimately aiming to gather the wisdom and strength to break our monsters and the monsters that oppose us. We have absolute control.

Me vs. Me

A war is inside my mind
Inside my mind I reside
To decide
Which side do I decide?
Can I even decide which side?
If I am at war with I
How do I win a war?
For which I must die to survive
If I imprison myself,
How can the one who imprisons me be so wise?
If I hide my own truths, how can I be free with only lies?
This is why I must arrive at a height
Where I see I'm too alive to be alive
Where I must die from too much life
So aware I'm unaware I'm going there
Too aware that they stare and I don't care
I don't dare, I don't share

Living in dreams that I keep
So far but so close that I reach
I am awake as I sleep
Which is not deep
But under the surface, from the surface it's deep
This struggle underneath
I beat to be beat
My victory is only defeat

Why do I not listen to what I hear?
Why do I think against my thoughts?
And why do I look for what I see
In a search to find I become lost
How do I ask of what I know?
How have I gone where I cannot go?
What is the answer to my question
If an answer is only a question?
When every lesson needs a lesson

How do I explain when that's what I'm trying to attain
How am I lost in a maze, in a maze that I made?
How can I not read this page
When I thought every phrase?

My heart is my weakness, my heart is my strength
My heart is my weapon, my heart is my pain
To gain is to lose
How are my losses my gains?
On the surface it is not waged
To aim at a vein would be in vain
No losses no gains
My mind is drowning, how is it in flames?
Burning with desires
To both feed, and smother the fire

Suicidal Killer

How do I die from what is living in me?
How are they lies, when it's what I believe?
How is it not there, when it's all I see?
Or is it there, when I cannot see?
That means it's not there to me
Like light does not exist to those who are blind
Light does not exist to those in the dark

How do I kill myself?
How does my enemy live within me?
How does he obey me, but betray me?
How do I make him, and he destroys me?
Am I not more powerful than he?
Is it not my being that allows him to be?
Why do I allow myself to lose me
To what he's beginning to be?
Why should I surrender to a beginner when I'm a winner?
And the war has just begun
Day after day, each day is a battle
Each battle I won
How can he kill me when I have his gun?
Should I shoot me to escape a torture,
From someone who is bound by my every command?
Why should I die at the hand of a man with no hands?

How do I kill what is living in me?
How do I find what I cannot see?
How can I search for what I've hidden from me?
He knows where I'll look; where I look he won't be
How do I find what is hiding in me?
How do I kill what is living in me
When I have defenses for attacks like these?

My heart has been hardened and locked with a key
Which I threw into the ocean, it's lost in the sea
My mind is so deep, I swim in the thoughts
Memories that had been lost, and lessons that cost
I think I might drown, then I hear a sound
Torpedo! Torpedo!
He's bringing me down!
But those are my weapons, and that is my ship
And every other thought he puts me against
This wall
He destroys with his ploys
When I dodge his dark noise
In the silence it's void
Now his missiles are duds, and the ship now a sub
And I submerge him, until he's lost like I was

Younger Me

I saw it all
Even what you still refuse to see
As if you can refuse it to be
I knew how uncomfortable you felt
But I could never comfort you
Those angry tears
I would only run from you
Things I was scared to feel
So scared of fear

To act as if everything's fine
But hoping someone would just pay attention
You need help, but no one can help you
You need help to ask for help too
I should've told them what I knew
I just thought I knew what that would do
I further damage you to not damage you
But ME TOO

Lifeguards all around
How can I drown and you can't see?
I scream, "Rescue me!"
To blind men who can see
Atheists pray for me
Asking a God they don't believe
Monsters they love and let go unchecked
Allowing him to bite my neck

I was there
I felt his stare
I felt his hands, those of a filthy man
I will never be clean again
Him with the two faces

Those smiles they give back to his
Make me sick, like when my back's to his
Slick tongue that stabs me for his quick come
I turned your back
I should have watched it for you
Abandoned in your silent cry
I only watched and let them ignore you
I wish to say this to set you free
—Forgive Me, Younger Me

Survivor

Muted news
I read captions of what I am to lose
This silent language should prepare me
I get ready
But I'm not ready
When my world shakes
I try to get a grip
But I'm hurled away

Silent earthquakes
Cracking my foundation
I fall and then my heart breaks
And where I used to take shelter, I can feel the rain
It comes in where the ceiling caved
Drowning as I pick up the pieces
When I go out to get some fresh air
I feel debris in all the breezes

Evidence everywhere, destruction so evident
Premonitions for the demolition
None of it makes sense
Everything of relevance is so irrelevant

But it will add up as it comes together
Once I rebuild, as I put it back together

Bittersweets

You make me so bitter, I can't taste the sweet
You make me so bitter, it taints all the sweets
I'm so bitter, it only wastes the sweets
But all I do is think of the sweets,
I can't stop thinking of sweets

Frozen in the door, getting chills from the ice
Drowning in the light, no
Nothing I like
How do I stand all these refrigerator fights?
I contemplate the milk, the struggle takes hours
I can't help but think of how you let it go sour
Pouring it isn't even half the battle
I even turn my nose up at the sight of cattle

Now all my tea has no sugar
All my coffee has no cream
I'm tired of this taste
I'm tired of twisting up my face
This sweetness I chase, I can never catch
Although it runs in place

I like to run, but I'm hesitant
You used to trip me for fun
Hunting is fun
But I'll never forget how you would shoot me with my gun
And water no longer soothes me
I remember how you used it to fill up my lungs

Everything great succumbs to the bitterness I taste
I might as well cut out my tongue
I won't be able to talk
But all I do with it anyway is complain to everyone

So the price to get rid of this bitterness left by you
Costs me part of me
It's either that, or forever eat
Bitter-sweets

Scars

What you don't want to show
Becomes the center of the scene, although hidden
Seeing you'd rather not be seen
You love shorts, but you settle for the long jeans
You hate to be covered by the seams
Because nothing is what it seems
But it shows,
How you show what you show
How you show what you don't
That mistake, nothing is what it seems

Those itches you have
Reflecting, reflexes
Forgetting not to scratch the scab
Pressing what's insecure
Pressure upon the Band-Aid
The curling tab
Washing around it, avoiding the area
Pressures to cover it up
Protecting the wound
Careful not to expose it too soon

Sometimes you need to let it breathe
The oxygen you need to receive
Kiss of the breeze
Mighty wind rubbing off on you
Might wind up rubbing off the scabs
The ones that overstay their welcome
Intimidating you to depend on its protection
That part of you no longer needs to be concealed
You will only see once it's peeled
That you are already healed
Even though the reminder is still there
Be reminded it's the pain you no longer have to feel

Entitled

War is forever
Though we think it never should be
A fallen angel's rule
A fallen world's rules
I've been through hell
Death by fire
I survive
Then
I burn alive

I was meant to die
And part of me did die
Where I was purified
Dropped jewel
War is forever
Battles that cure me
To no end
Enduring
Someone burned my house down, someone pulled me
From the rubble, just to throw me back into the fire

See nobody will help, everybody only wants to see me die
My thoughts cry, but my heart would love to see them try
Cool exterior, but I'm burning up inside
In this confusion, a gun is a solution
Delusions
My focus on this darkness is only keeping me in its midst,
In its pits
Devoured by what worries me,
My mind stays on what's hurting me
Put myself in a prison for those who want to murder me
And I'm a sacrifice for those who turn on me
Retaliation seems to be the only thing holding me
As betrayal seems to try to take my soul from me

Came with a fistful
Was left with bite marks on my hand
But you betray me once, you won't betray me again
Betray me, betray yourself in the end
Now that I've lost it all, ask me what I think of my friends
It wasn't hard to be loyal back then
Friends to the end
I've seen those friendships end
Hard to say that I knew it back then
Hard to explain what I was feeling back then
Even all that money wasn't fulfilling back then
How much of me I gave to get it back then
Then to throw it all away,
I can't let myself feel that way again

I return to living water those thieves been fishing in
I refuse to bite their bait
Finding myself is to reel it back in
I remove the hook
Where I'm meant to sink, I swim
Remove the limits so I see no end
I removed the glass ceiling I was feeling boxed-in
I removed the shades and I no longer have to squint at the light
Remove the gloves, they're bound too tight
Now I'm bound to bound through what's bound, in my might
In their sight
No longer going round and round
No longer is there competition
It's no longer a fight

The dark warriors are shaken, all have heard of me
My heel dug into the breast of adversity
The belt of truth in my upraised fist
Here you see a champion
—Spiritual warfare

TAME
bringing something uncontrollable or intolerable into a submissive or manageable state

Thanks to You

Look at me now
Like you looked at me then
Look at me now, like you looked at me when I fell down
Like you looked down
Like you looked down at the ground
Like you looked down and greeted me with your frown

Look at me now
Like you looked at me then
When my frown made you grin
When my low head raised your chin
Look at me now, like you looked at me then
When you thought then you were looking at my end

Look at me now
Like you looked when my defeat made you proud
When your laughter was loud
Like when you laughed with the crowd; them all pointing down
The points poking me, prodding me
I remember the sound
Like strong winds meant to blow me down
But it also made the fire growl
The fire forged what you see now

So look at me now
Like you looked when you saw me last
Why have you hidden your laugh?
Your frown is so much different
I can no longer see your teeth
Like my grief that didn't last
Your high chin now low in a mask

Look at me now, like you did in the past
Your eyes hide behind their lids as I pass
You can't see me as I pass, won't see me as I pass
Don't want to see me pass
You blink as I pass

When other thoughts pass, and you think of how I passed
And you can't think of how I passed
And you want to ask how I passed, I've already gone past
Leaving you in my past

Why did you not look?
You thought I would laugh as I passed?
As I laugh at my past
It's funny how I last to pass
Past at last
And did not pass my last
And not the last to pass
Thanks to you

> Patience is valuable in struggle, just as much as tactics (if not more). In everything, endurance counts most when unaccounted for, the unexpected in the underestimated.
>
> In all opposition, we must bring forth the vaccine from the virus.
>
> In all struggle, we must bring forth the diamond from the pressure.

10.

Mental Work

#2148629 #21456172

Awareness invades me
My senses become alive
Resurrected from a death
That went unnoticed
My eyes become flooded with light
Illumination of truth's life
Leading me
Guiding me where I will be
Fulfilling my purpose

It's time to focus.

Once we realize that our thinking processes—or our *unawareness* of our thinking processes—create the circumstances in our lives, we understand that we are the cause. There is a higher power that is to be found within ourselves. We must only depend on God—on the source, on our subconscious treasury—for the inspiration necessary to secure a solid, reliable cause and vision, to change unfavorable conditions and to form an ideal life. Awareness of this truth allows us to grow and be spiritually strengthened without limit by our higher power. When we reach the point of absolute faith—without the shadow of a doubt existing in our spirit—we are on the brink of freedom, enveloped in truth, love, and positivity. This is a force to be unrivaled by resistance.

We are to use this energy to expiate in re-creation. Your first intention should be to expel the remnant of negative causes within you, that harmful, habitual thinking your subconscious has soaked up and distributed throughout your life experience. Behold a new thought! It's that simple.

It's simple, but not easy. The difficulty is in the struggle that ensues, the double-mindedness that attempts to dissipate this new mind and block liberation. Focus. Hold onto the faith that empowers your new causes. Manifest new effects to bring NEW life.

Get Up

You hearing you say you are damaged
Only damages more
Pent up pain
Pouring from your soul
Commence disdain

Just let it pour, out of your pores
But don't sweat it
If it has you floored, just get off the floor
Because you're not damaged
You're just sore

And you are not damaged
You are not in need of repair
Like your clothes with their tears
From every wear everywhere
Be aware,
That's a lot of wear
Just find something else to wear

Stuck in your stare
Into unnecessary cares
Worries you can't smother with your glare
Only flare what is there,
And what is not there
You may curse the curse
But then you dwell in the spell

I've never been hurt
I've only been sore
The clothes always tear
But they are there to wear
—And tear

And every time I end up sore
Then I just heal myself more
I've never noticed a loss
I just always know I want more

I don't count the score, I just aim to score
So what your clothes tore!
That's what new clothes are for
Why are you still on the floor?!
What are your wings for?
When you don't fly you're a wasted sore
Because when you're meant to fly,
You're meant to soar

Spread your wings . . .

Image

Why does she cry?
She is too beautiful to see less out of those eyes
Those eyes, that sparkle from her tears as she cries
So beautiful
I wonder what's inside

Wondering what's inside that makes her cry
Does she weep because she has something she cannot keep?
I wonder upon this wonder as I watch her cry

How can something so ugly come from something so beautiful?
Is it because the beautiful define the ugly?
But ugliness from ugliness cannot regress it
Unless she lets it
Oh yes, beauty is pleasant
Although they stress it,
They seem to not know they cannot possess it
It is a position it is not a possession
Though it possesses
Ugliness derives from beauty
What they feel when they can't claim it,
What they will do to attain it
Pretty faces turn ugly just to gain it,
Attempt, but can't take it
Then they become uglier in an attempt to fake it
Or they hope to make their ugly break it

Is she broken, is that why she cries?
Is it the lies from the pressure inside?
Or is it the pressure that lies, the pressure to lie?
But the truth lies in the lies, see how she cries
It all comes out
I watch her, wondering if that's why

Lie to her face to lie by her side
Then lie on her when pushed aside

When she pulled out the truth that was pushed under lies
But beauty is too true
What is the ugly to do, but to try to put the ugly in you?
That's when the ugly comes out,
She's just pushing all ugliness out
She births pride, lust, greed, all that evil needs
To steal for, to kill for, to kill just to steal her
Things that no longer thrill her
She didn't ask for this life,
Sometimes they make her feel so wrong in her right

So, Beautiful, is that why you cry?
So beautiful, Beautiful is that why you hide?
You know what you cause with that face you no longer like,
Like they like
Is your crying your cause to defile a beauty so liked?
Why do you surrender,
When you can't lose a fight?
Like light can't lose to night
Don't cut off the light

You only know how it works
You only know how it is seen
You are more than just a thing
The witch that holds the worse curse
The angel that brings extreme dreams
See, you don't know the true power of beauty,
You don't know what beautiful means

It's not meant to let them influence your cause
Let your cause influence
Don't let ugliness defile you, when you can make plenty so pretty
I don't like to see you cry, Beautiful
Smile
So you can make me smile Beautiful

Swan

There is no truth in what they say
Don't you see the truth in what they say?
It's ok, you're just blending in
You ugly girl, it's an ugly world
You fit right in

You are enough,
You are worth too much to give it up
To be what they don't see
Because they don't see
Overseers that don't look enough
Keeping you under them
You weren't meant to swim amongst them
There is more to life
Why wait for it to dawn on shallow ponds?
The light first hits the mountain's height
Eagles are so much higher up
So stop looking up to that stupid duck

Take advantage and see the advantages you can take
All things of which you can think
As she worries about her pretty face
What you can find, if you take your time
That one of a kind, that beautiful mind
Make me smile, make me laugh,
Open me up, it's all about what's inside
Just make sure you stop all the ugly thoughts
Don't let them tear apart that beautiful heart

Don't think being ugly is the only way
Be what you want to be
Show the world what you want them to see
You should affect the world, the world should not affect you
Whose eyes are closer to you?
Who can see you better than you?
They don't know what they speak of
Fill their eyes with images of their mind
Make their lips turn on themselves
Telling themselves what they tell on themselves
Until they confess:
The ugliness I see is because of the ugliness in me
You are beautiful
Don't be fooled by a fool's eyes
Don't corrupt that beautiful mind

Opinions aren't facts
But what you think is . . . is

Philosophy

Chrome guns and soft roses
Gleaming and rotten
The steel remains as life passes away
The killers watching the living die
Shit under the flies
What lives behind the eyes?
All that shit, all those lives
All those eyes
Shifting their sights of chambers
Before a decorated bed of roses

Life imitates art
God is an artist
But he wraps me in a carcass
Adam framed me
My mother raised me
But the world made me
Corruption

It doesn't matter what you place on my plate
When my mind is hungry
Consumption
You are the only one who talks to me
Your words aren't up for discussion
I don't realize you wear a mask
I've never seen another person
Default perceptions
I never knew another version
My clarity is distortion
My mind a person, this force an extortion

All white rooms
All black surburbans
Windowless walls and blindfolds

How do I keep my head above water?
Concrete tugging on my toes
The sea of humanity covers me up
Confined to the ocean floor
Prisoner of war

It was only a tub!
Says the drain, unplugged
Tainted water drains

A penetrating doubt
From rounds of truth
The battle it struggles to begin
But the war it will win
Earning nothing
After losing everything
—Square one

Suppressors

Hidden meanings, true enough
Suited thugs, confuse enough
Muted slugs, costumes on thugs
Corporate covers

Silenced by suppressors
Feeding me mothballs,
Wishing I would choke on these mothballs
But I have a mind
No I'm sorry! I don't have a mind

I have a copy machine
Spitting out what's pushed upon me
I don't plan my plans
As they scan what they plan
Holding me captive, are slaves until I release
They wait as I captivate
To be captors of what I make with relief
That the printer of the print doesn't see
But who needs eyes, saving memory
Keeping my cards close

Playing dumb, as I tamper with guns
Until it backfires on them
Until I've won

Talk

All things you can't contain
Things that stop you up
Things you need to drain
Things that shift with your shape
Formed to what you make
What do you make of it?

Words are like water
Let your ears drink of life
Let life drown your sorrow
Denounce death in spirit
Speak of the feeling from the filling
Empty out your heart
Speak so they can feel it
But don't speak what brings a grimace
Don't speak of limits
Don't try to bring attention to every blemish, facing life
Start each sentence for a win at the finish
Speak your victory into existence

Don't taint the water
Don't serve me poison
My every sense rejects it
But I see how you accept it
No matter how I tell it
The antidotes neglected
Continue to be hurt by those words
They talk so much shit
You're so used to bathing with turds
I try to rinse you with this water
It's foreign
You don't understand it
You don't know how to accept what you heard
I'm speaking another language

Just getting your feet wet
The water's just fine
Led by the divine
To accept this fine wine
A sip may be enough
You may get full off of one cup
Good spirits
Feel good from good feelings
Digesting expressions
Except exceptions
Massages of the temples
Visions in the temple
Meditate as you verbally mediate
Supernatural messages to the mental

Let stresses of the future be the past
Loosening the tense
Moving you stiffs, move in the gifts
Present to uplift
So listen up
To live it up
Get back on your feet
As I drop the mic
Applaud to life

Heart

That thing that never falters
That thing that keeps you going
What you see ahead of you is damned,
But somehow it keeps on flowing
That warmth inside, when outside it's snowing
Darkness falls all around you,
But you keep on glowing

No one else can see
But you're just knowing
That pull that pushes
The strength that gives strength
The strength that attracts the weak
The drip of crimson on the pale pink
Like the swift creek to the dry teak
Firmly ground like gritted teeth
Pulling all you got, to push

It beats like the winner
Triumphs over losses
Unless you are drawn across to the lost

It will spread what poison is drawn in
Be careful of what you allow to be consumed
To assume the steady rhythm, to beat the best
—Care to keep a good heart

Meant

Reflecting on your thoughts
Talking to yourself
Listening to your words
Karma's absurd
You never get what you deserve
You seem to never achieve
But for some reason, somehow you still believe
Never stop believing

All you can do is you, just do you
Stay true to find truth
It reveals itself
It's that way for a purpose, like your purpose
Stop trying to reveal it yourself
A volunteer for the magician
But he doesn't need your help

Running from the rain
You run to the desert, it's overcast
Predicting the weather
Based on whatevers
Clouding your judgment, you can't see the light
It's like concealing yourself

Missing what's for you
Passing judgment on your current
Lost at sea
Lost, searching for something new
When something new is coming to you
But passing you up, as you look back
As you do the math for your future
Trying to add up your past

Keep your head up
Even when you're tired and it's tough to do
Keep your eyes open for the present
So you can see what's in front of you

MENTAL WORK
Constructive, intellectual activity directed by a strong will to strive for a healthier lifestyle

Perfection

Confidence without judgment is foolery.
Strength without measurement is consequential.
Power without responsibility is destructive.
Mind without the heart is misleading.
Heart without the mind is confusion.
Body without the soul is void.
A spirit confined is a prison for the mind.

If you don't acknowledge your wants,
You'll never recognize your needs.
If you never give, you will never receive.
If you never imagine, you will never believe.
Use it or lose it.

You must reach to touch to feel, you must listen to hear,
And you must look to see.

Truth is the king each lie must bow to.
You must know the truth in order to lie, you don't make the lie.
For it is the truth that makes the lie,
Not just makes you make the lie.

You tailor the lie according to the truth you want to hide
And the truth is the reason why you lie—
Whatever deceitful motive you may have
So therefore all lies are subject to the truth

You must destroy to create, you must create to destroy.

Be without fear, but not without sense.
Being scared and being cautious are two different things.
Being timid and being careful are two different things.

Perfection is impossible,
Embracing and utilizing imperfection
Makes a person, who cannot be perfect, the perfect person.
Perfectly imperfect.

Do not yield to weakness.
Do not lose yourself in your flaws – denial.
Do not fall between those cracks,
They are part of your identity.
By learning your way around them,
Navigating the mind, learning ways to fill the cracks;
They are lessons in themselves.
For what fills them are characteristics on their own.
The weaknesses illuminating the strengths.
The best part of you is how you handle the worst parts.
Better yourself!

There is no feeding a mind that doesn't hunger. Desire is the catalyst to fulfillment. Desire ignites drive; discernment is the "key" to desire; discernment also powers your "navigation." Desire is constant; reborn, renewed. We should never be what we want to see, always see more. We should always see who we are to be; we should never stop growing. We should forever desire to see more, striving for constant elevation. Seeking an air above this altitude.
—Forever Better

11.

Overcoming
#5942496 #59486298

I left my pain behind
But my pain hasn't left me
I have to let go
I have to overcome in my mind
I have to overcome my thoughts

I have to get over it

When we overcome, sometimes we've just won a battle but have yet to win the war. In reflection—identifying resistance through failure, disappointment, and obstacles—we can move forward more wisely. We must let our past be our guide; let our victory be our blueprint.

The awareness of our power prepares us for the jungle ahead, with its pits of emotional quicksand. As we climb out of the valley up the high mountain, the world will be spread before us, revealing the bigger picture with absolute clarity. This time you will know the terrain. With confidence, you will point into the horizon, scouting a new direction.

This new vision reaches to the very core of ourselves, where we will discover an untapped power within us. This new vision also enables us to see through people, to the parts they don't even see. Not that they are flawed, just simply unaware. We will distinguish the reasons behind and relationships between each cause and effect to identify the source of our affliction in all things. The application of this knowledge to our causes is our ability to separate from dysfunctional habits, relationships, and situations. We will cut off these issues at the root. We'll learn to leave all of the baggage behind and purge any and all dysfunction—Permanently.

Remember Me?

Memories pick at me
I wonder if you remember me
Would you remember me?
Could you remember me, buried deeply in your memories?
Remember when your eyes met mine, and you shuddered?
Then you stuttered, like I . . . I . . .
Remember me?

The one who introduced you to love
Remember when you told me you'd never forget
Remember me?

The one who rescued you from your depression,
The one who fought with your worrying
Remember me?

The one who never judged your confessions
The one who wrestled with your insecurities
Remember how much I would stress from you stressing
And how I would strengthen you against your enemies?

Remember how you felt so weak, and how I made you strong?
Remember how I made it right every time you were wronged?
Remember how they made you feel like you didn't belong,
How I opened up my world so you could fit in?
Remember, you told me you thought you weren't pretty enough?
I hope you remember to never say that shit again!
Remember the days before we built your confidence,
When you were so affected by comments?
Remember when you stopped it;
Sometime after I made them stop it?
You asked me how I made them stop,
And I made you change the topic
Remember, you told me with me you felt safe,
With me there is no other place?
Remember how you lied to my face?

Remember?
Remember you said there was nobody else,
But I had to learn the truth from everybody else?
I remember, but I wish I forgot
But I still remember
I would take you to dinner
You weren't worth it to them, no one ever took you out
I remember you didn't even know your worth
But even then I had no doubt

I'll always remember your smile
How could I ever forget!
So much laughter it would make us feel sick!
So much joy, we couldn't come up with a wish!

I remember how you would cry
I couldn't stand that look in your eyes
I couldn't leave your side until you were healed inside
I remember how you would never let go,
How every depart was so slow
Remember?

Remember all those late nights and early mornings?
The sunrises; the sunsets?
And how every time a day would begin,
The feeling wishing it would never end?
Remember me? Am I even in your memories?
Remember you had nobody, and you said I was all you had?
Remember you had nothing, remember all I went and got?
I put it all on the line for you
Remember how I took that loss?
Remember how long we fought; remember how hard I fought?
Not hard enough,
Then you said you had enough
You said that I didn't have enough, and that you needed a lot
But, remember
All the things that you said you would always remember?
I guess not,
Or you probably just forgot!

Limits

So optimistic to start ignitions, seeing perfect conditions
Peeling out, taking off the layers
Your pleas to slow down when the rain comes
Your piercing screams when we start skidding

Looking up to me, seeing everything you need to see
Feeder to my highways
Onto living life the freeway
To spread your wings
Deployed spoilers on the Autobahn
The highest volume for your favorite song
Nothing less than everything
And everything you need to hear,
And everything you need to feel
Touching redlines before I change gears
Push it

To the limits that don't exist
Those walls I always vault
Those doors I always kick
Down is like a sling
—Shot—
Down is landing on a trampoline

Those obstacles you let intimidate you
Those obstacles I see as exercise
I'll hike waterfalls, I'll climb skies
I'll melt the artic, I'll freeze hell
I'll drive with no wheels, I'll fly with no wings
I don't care what comes
As long as your love comes with it

But too bad your love has limits

Tease

And you just leave me here
With your scent on my skin
And your taste on my tongue
This race you challenged me to,
But you refused to run
As I fight the burn in my lungs
This heart of mine races
Passing all these places
To be number one

Craving a trophy
I could have never won
No point in what I've done
Taking shots, then seeing there is no goal
Practicing for playoffs for championships that don't exist

What's the point of taking the next step if it leads off a cliff?
After living this life on the edge
My hopes are too high
I push myself too far
Down to the bottom line
Stranded in a strand of difference
I can no longer fall
For the kiss convince
Your synthetic presence
Erasing essence
Killing what you birth
As I enjoy what hurts

Fingertips outstretched
Reaching for what's left, gasping for that last breath
That last look into those eyes, as they darken
As this love dies

Without You

Groping in the dark for my fallen star
Fallen wishes upon shooting stars
Someone shot my sun out of the sky
Where has my day gone? There becomes a knight in me

Time flies, but I never believed you would take off
All this time I put in
Still I wear my watch that no longer ticks, crooked
Crossed eyes that are still looking
Over it
Time to close the curtains on the windows you won't look in

Closing my eyes
Your love is so blind
All the things I see that you never know
I look so high I never see that it keeps you so low

I close my eyes
Love is blind
Pictures of you that my soul won't let go
Images of you draped in my diamonds and gold
Earthly treasures on my heart that I couldn't let go
My heart couldn't take the weight
Ensuring strokes upon the pain I face
I didn't think you would break

You let me down
But you forced me to acknowledge mistakes
Stakes that you couldn't take
I now realize a mortal's forever and always
Teasing my eternal state
I can no longer wait at a wake for you to awake
I must now face this fate
Without my heart

I'm so heartless

You were my heart
How can a man with no heart feel at home even at home?
Opening doors to memories of you
Doors I quickly close
Seeing my heart isn't here
What are your eyes to see when your mind is closed?
The birth of dark, here it starts
Here you don't have to see you're alone
What are you to do once you refuse to see light?
Isn't a diamond only but a stone?

Why is it that beauty cannot be unshown?
When you close your eyes you see the imprint on your soul
It's up to you if it fades or if it glows
The highs or lows they chose
And those they never chose
Because they never chose
Some have been buried and some rose,
And some have been buried with a rose
Though some have been buried and still arose

Fighting dying to the death
Decaying for a breath
To find life after death
Asking yourself why you cried for what you left
Reflections of growing
Now that you have grown
Up to the mirror to be shown
Where alone isn't alone

Once you see that all you see isn't all there is to see
I close my eyes to open my mind to see all that I am
And all that I am to be
Without you

My Fly-By Bye

The whole time you were with me
You only sought what I've always seen
I thought you were here for me
Around the time the vision came around
You were looking down
You couldn't stay around
You couldn't stay down

With nobody to pick me up (including you)
All I could do was walk
Too slow for you
It didn't take long
I found out what you're about

Now I no longer have to talk
And I no longer have to hear you when you shout
You with all that doubt
'N me with all this clout
Now you're without a route
You burned that bridge down
And aimed your flamethrower at me
When I tried to put the fire out

You cut me off in a choice of choppers
You left in the hog
You didn't see the helicopter
So I'm not stopped by what stops yours
Reminded of the lesson, looking at the ground
I see you need to be rescued from that burning bridge
But I won't let you bring me back down

Now your shouts aren't as loud,
The rotors drown the sound,
As you attempt to wave me down, jumping up and down
Stuck behind that firewall
You can be mistaken as a mime

You boxed yourself in
You may be worth a dime
You might see change from me
But I won't drop a line
No,
You can't even reach my line
I can't come back for you
I've already wasted too much time
You used to look down on me, now you look up to me
As I dip my nose down into the sky

OVERCOMING

to conquer any opposing force by mental effort and moral strength

12.

Love Life
#7492187 #74991275

A twinge of guilt
I accuse the innocent
Love is not the culprit
The one who uses love wrongly
The abuse of love
Though lovers are flawed
Love is perfect

It is this I open up to

Don't be ashamed to love, and do not ever be afraid to love.

If someone has done you wrong, that is not on you; that is on them. They misused your love. They are at fault. You did not make a mistake by loving. In the same way, if someone gives me money and I am robbed, I don't regret accepting the money. I don't think, "I should be broke from now on so that nobody else can rob me!" Or if I lose my job, I don't reason, "I won't look for another job because I'll probably get laid off there too."

The appropriate response to being robbed or laid off is to move on and surely continue accepting money or looking for a job opportunity. So why would we not be open to a new relationship? Receive love like you would receive money, like you would receive that new job. Always be open to love, without forfeiting wisdom—Remain Positive.

Love Songs

All of these love songs
Making my love strong
Turned on a love song
And turned my love on
Feeding the fire, starving desire

She makes me feel like a love song
Like my life is my most loved song
Makes me fantasize that it comes along
Makes me realize I've been loved wrong
Or maybe that I've loved wrong

She makes me want to sing a love song
My heart would like to sing along
But in my mind I may sing it wrong
Like the love, harmony not lasting long
Like my mind and my heart don't get along
Still blaming each other for the love gone

She makes me want to write a love song
I need something to put all this love on

New Love

Empty promises
Or you don't know what honest is
I asked for dedication
You asked for an explanation
It ended up being a persuasion
Then came commitment
Then you started acting different

Is it my false trust,
Or the truth you cover up?
Why are you giving up?
Throwing in the towel
This is where time will get you
Down to the bare essentials
Lies I know I smelled
Time will tell
Exposure

Feelings in the nude
Facing the mirror of my mind
Erika Badu and the smoke infused
This baggage you left me
Calling on Tyrone
The calls won't go through
My thumb hovers over the screen, no
I won't call you

Flying phone
I run back to
What did I do?
The shake of the head
The downward sighs
What do I do?

Loves of this life leave me confused
Leave me free to choose
Leaving me locked down
To the cell that you sell out
The key is you, and you leave
And this is what you leave me to
You never see me through

So many eyes
Which should I try?
The pair that won't so much as blink at the roaring river
That water you left under that charred bridge
Your Rubicon flooding my route

Looking for a new point of view
I need somebody to help me figure it out
The one that sees a sea
And swims with me
Towards a shore hidden by distance
Only to be discovered in time
Only to be reached by faith
And ready to give whatever it takes

So what is a river?

Losing Love

Secrets that I forgot
Life that was never lost
I would love to be reminded
Been so long since I've been excited
That look in those eyes that never dies
You survived
Behind enemy lines
This search that took so much time

Captured by the lies
Hidden truths
Camouflage, uniform blending mirage
Seeing what I don't see
Perceptions induced by misdirection
Not seeing what I see
I gave up, I thought you were gone

You never gave up all along
Waiting for me to find a way
As my impatience moved me on to finer things
So fake behind these fine lines
No comfort in the nighttime
I need my old tattered blanket
Coldness of the memory
The absence of the warmth that made it

Things you show that they could never know
The confused witnesses to the lost battles
Uncontained laughter at the codes
These inside jokes that seem so sacred

The rituals that remind you
That I will find you
Reminding me to find you
Reminding me why I still have to try
Reminding me of your strength
Reminding me that you will never die

Indescribable

When you smile, the sun shines
But when you cry, it rains
I can't die from the bad weather
Only because I live for the days
Sometimes you drive me crazy with your twisted ways
When the road gets rough, the passenger also complains
An annoyance just the same
A speed bump on every block
Every time we move on, it's like something makes us stop
But as long as we can go
Even though it may be slow

I see your head drop
I see your shoulders slump, like the world's on top
My hand under your chin, I push for uplifted thoughts

And there's something always here
Like something I always hear
Like encouragement not to fear
Like sometimes I hate work, then payday is here
But like payday is always near
Like we pay with our tears
Like what a deal; it was worth way more than some tears!

And as I raise your chin,
I look into your eyes
There goes that thing I can't describe
And then you say "I love you"
Then I know why
—It's Indescribable

Values

And look we're still here
I see you still there
All ways, like always
When it all leaves, you're always left
You alone, so I won't be alone
I'm never disowned,
No matter what I don't own

But what do I need?
When you're my everything
I have everything in you
You keep me going, you're my fuel
I burn with passion,
The power of a million stallions
To make flames roar from the exhaust
But we're never exhausted

A fire that never goes out
I can't fight it
Even if I pull up to the hydrant and bring the hose out
Ashes like afterthoughts
The messes we can wipe away
Sacrificed what once seemed important
Things
I no longer use to boast
Celebrations, broken glass
Looks like I burned the toast
They say that's why they never come over
Never disowning our imperfections
At least we saved our old beloved malfunctioning toaster

LOVE LIFE

an expression for the romantic relationships between lovers

13.

The Blessing and the Curse
#6842731 #68417342

No one bothered to lift me up
I was at the bottom
I felt pain in its full measure
It enveloped me, it was a part of me
I came to know pain intimately
I came to understand it
I came to this understanding
To come to be understanding
To bless others by my escape from this curse

This I will not run from
This I cannot run from
This is how I relate to the struggle
My heart will always ache

I can never forget pain

In hardship, struggle, and resistance, there is a point when you feel you're at the bottom. It is there where you feel the pain in full measure, enveloping you, becoming part of you. As you feel it, you come to know it, and as you come to know it, you come to understand it.

This deepest dip in the valley is the point just before you start to climb. On your way up and out, recognize that your past is the past. Just because it built you doesn't mean it defines you. You have wisdom now, an invaluable asset that should be used, not resented. You have come to understanding to come to *be* understanding—to make a difference in the lives of others.

We are one spirit. Our individual growth and progress should produce growth and progress for all. Our testimony alone can uplift, enlighten, advise, and serve as righteous direction. The wisdom of our experiences can be implemented in others' lives to help them avoid negative circumstances. Let us be helpful, not hurtful, refusing to subject others to what we were subjected to. They don't deserve to go through hell just as much as we didn't deserve it. When possible, let us empathize for and protect others in difficult situations.

Do something. Be somebody to somebody.

Fallen Star

Wonder how we reach the heavens
All the space in between, full of darkness
All the storms in between, those twists the wind blows
It's raining stars

The trajectory of fallen stars,
The angles we can only pretend to fathom
Digging into the depths of the concrete jungle
The dirt that seeps into their surface as they climb that rut

Stepping over those cracks in the sidewalk
Without actually knowing why
Without the slightest wonder as we pass another by
A world you never had to see
Grateful, you never knew to be

Shooting stars you wished upon
Twinkles fading beneath bitten dust
Fallen stars, you just move along
Even though you used to sing along
You just move along
As if they never sang a song

Fall from Grace

I took a leap of faith
Maybe my faith wasn't in the right place
I look up, but they never reach down
They turn their mouths up in distaste
I guess no one wants to be associated
With the man with the dirt on his face

Do I disgrace you with my disgrace?
Maybe after all, love really isn't so great
Or maybe after all, I was played in our trade
And your love was really just fake
Like I was fully committed,
But they were really just dates
You didn't have my back
At least it can relate
To my heart when it breaks

I can't get back up
The pain has me stuck
Some old man keeps me company
He says his name is Chuck
There is nobody else
And Chuck cannot help
He told me down here in this rut,
They all will disown me,
He talks like he knows me

Tears blur my vision,
The sweat of the lonely
But somehow I find courage
Maybe from looking at Chuck so discouraged
To end up like him is my worry
I call out, no one's worried
I contemplate my fate
My head starts spinning
So now my emotions are stirring

In this world a blender
Buttons pushed, emotional triggers
Here at the bottom where it hurts me
Where I only hear what hurts me . . .

Then I hear a voice . . .
Then I say hurry . . .
As I'm bleeding out, grieving
He lifts me up with his mercy
—My fall from grace

Verdict

In your hands my life is a manila tab
In your hands my life is letters on a notepad
Scribbled by a part-time drunk who never knew me
Only heard about me from an addict who will use me
To escape punishment for his using
You know they are abusing
But I get no justice,
You let them abuse me

How can you judge partial
In your hands my life is partial
In your hands my life is a particle
You just wash your hands
In your life your hands cleared an obstacle
Avoiding doing your duty

I find the jury guilty
To vote for a man not running
For a position that doesn't fit him
To take a stand to be knocked down
All this stands on a stand
For a clown

I'm joining the circus now
I'm led to an animal's cage
These chains induce an animal's rage

All for this witless witness
I want you to witness this
Since you are so fond of witnessing
I need you to witness this
Remember, I was opposed by witnesses
But I don't have a witness
And I'm sure not one to witness

I only give testimony to God in a cell
I say he let me down
But I see I'm down in a well
Well away from those who tell me to rise
To make sure I fell
But not for them
For on my knees
I can finally please

Now pride is not as high as me
Looking down
Looks so much like bribery
Someone's buying testimonies
Someone's selling me, but I can't sell out
Someone's selling freedom
Someone's buying their life back
With the life of their friends
So he's more fit for society
Than the one who accepts the consequence
Who can tell me this makes sense?
Only those who can tell me they know
It's not about what I owe
It's not about my soul
It's about what they stole
Conviction

Making convictions but having none
Saving the world from the truth with the lies they run
How can they right wrongs, when their rights are wrong?
The right to wrong those who do wrong,
Because they don't have the right
Who will right these wrongs?

Where is this witness now?
Where they have their hands in it
This is where they place their hands over his eyes

Here he's unaware of his whereabouts
He's on a leash but they say they're guides
To what they want him to see
But this is not a surprise
This is taking lives

That perception, that direction, that point, that deception
Because the surface yields no clues that you can use
To ordain a depth you can't construe
You won't view the deep, if you won't deepen your view
Pronouncing words you don't know the meaning of
Saying things you don't mean to
How can you explain what you see,
Without understanding what it can be?
Like a sailor who knows the sky
Like an aviator who knows the sea
Like you who knows me

Do you know my intent?
Like a sailor knows a plane
Like an aviator knows a ship
How can you feel what I feel?
How can you think my thoughts?
How can you decide my decision?
How do you determine intent?

You judge Sully's vision
But you couldn't plan a better plan than his improvisation
You say you wouldn't have hit that iceberg
Like that was E.J. Smith's intention
But you make a decision based on what you see on the surface
When you don't look that deep
From this broken vessel where you're letting lives sink
How do you know what you know?
What do you know about how you know?
What do you know?
How do you know?

I want you to witness this witness live this
But then they would want a new witness
You can't have what you never got, so how did you get this
—Verdict?

In My Shoes

No way
To walk in my shoes
For those not prepared to take theirs off
Those soles soft
When those souls are off, when those soles are off

And those cold winds, the frostbite
And those rough roads
That are rough on purple toes
And those hot suns
The ones that make you want to run, and not want to run
Worn treads that make you slip when it's slick
The bottoms are thin, so those feet ache
Still a ways to go
After you've gone all that way

Squinting at the horizon, your hand the only shade
Standing where you can't stay
Those monsters await, just past the snapping snakes
You want to sit, but this ain't the place
Those fears that come alive, and mutate from polluted lakes
To stagnate
Exiled to wastelands

Was wasted
Carried to the trashcan, pushed down

Now back on my own two feet
The evasion
Your exclamation of damnation
You never take your time to rinse off such a perfect creation
Misdirection and error, is as a language misspoken
And dirty does not mean broken
Your birds-eye view of me in trenches
Your judgement of choices you never had to make
Chances you say you'd never take
Chances you never had to take

Bible Thumper

You say I need salvation
I say I need an explanation
You say you had a revelation
But all you talk about is damnation
Secretly this is your examination
This is your contamination
This is my lamentation
How can you be reading without seeing?

Why are you always talking and never listening?
Why do you always tell me which way I should go?
Knowing I already know
Why do you never ask how I got here?
Why do you tell me why I'm here,
But you never ask me what I'm looking for?
Why do you tell me what I need to find,
When you don't know what I lost?

Why are you always preaching but never teaching?
Why are you talking about places you will never show me?
You tell me I have to get there, but not how to get there
How can you tell me how to get there,
And you don't know where I am?
I see you don't know where I'm coming from
How can you see the bad in me and not see the good?
You use the bad against me,
You never show me what my good will do for me

You want me to listen, but you ignore me
What an example you are
I can see the light from the windows of my soul,
But the house is barred
With my spirit choking, how can you hear a response?
My captors keep me away
Like kidnappers, they have me hidden away
You claim I'm lost, but you never look for me
All you do is open up a book for me

Abandoned

Now raise your hand if you've felt pain
Even though every hand in the world is raised
These collective palms still won't block out the sun
The light still bursts through the cracks of darkness
Like these fingers we can't fully close

The way we see the light when our eyes are closed
That hope stirring our thoughts, dragging us out
When our mind is closed
That glow underneath that locked door

Illuminated corridors
Soles leaving impressions upon the glowing floors
Seeing their shadows come and go
To humble yourself
Adjusting your sight lower than low
Hoping to face toes
Desperate knows
Someone has the key to set you free
Callused knuckles continue knocking
Have you ever been helpless?
Have you ever been helpful?

Your Spoiled Desire

Do you fall to the sky?
Do you rise to the floor?
Direction
Who will humble the rich?
Who will boast for the poor?
Boldness
What winner will cheat to even the score?
What defeat will achieve an award?
Selflessness

Finding the words
Hearing that small voice
Using that voice
To talk over pride
As it falls
Exposing the weakness it hides
The fear of the strong that survive
The strength it tries to hide
Fearing the humble that are to rise

I was telling lies to the truthful
Being true to the liars
Putting out the water, drinking from the fire
Burned by the liars
I was in a wreck, but I was not the driver

Now I would take the high road
But I see no road higher
I don't waste time looking ahead
I focus on the current, and balance on the wire

They joke and they laugh at me up here struggling
I laugh, despite my mood
But not because it's funny
I laugh for the fools with the food
Things that we will do when we're hungry

Your words would discourage me
But I can't see the inscriptions
I'm blind with ambition

You push the braille upon me
But all I feel is tension
Sparking my ambition, now sparkling with persistence
Your discussion of limits
I'm not deaf, I don't listen
Interrupted
My mind always mentions my lack of vision
Blind ambition

You hide mines in my path that I disarm
Loss of vision strengthens all other senses
Now your mines are mine
You supply my ammunition
With your full plate you taunt me
Why must you starve me?
You charge me up
I blow your charges on your warehouse
A need for a taste
That garnered
Now it garners your garnering
Things you will do when you're starving

Things you will do to those who starve you
In the name of hunger, let there be no mercy on you
Survival is vital, no thing you won't do just to eat

Sit the bitter at tables, fill the tables with sweets
Things I'll do once I eat
I would have done this for you
These things surely I'll do
Now that I have food

A BLESSING AND A CURSE
something that seems negative but in time reveals a positive purpose

14.

Free Me
#9412491 #94124917

Free me, Lord! Free me, Lord,
From the pressure of these manacles
Chained by the veil of Your parables
Free my spirit, Lord
From that which keeps me conformed to the world
The dark force is holding me behind limits preordained
These limits are only sustained because such hasn't been rebutted
Theories unchallenged, facts unproven

I am aware You are my power
I must seek You in all I do
Bless me with the power to seek this power
To be in power, to be empowered
To be consumed in absolute Truth

Bless me with the power to escape this weakness
Which is merely an illusion
My inner enemy in clandestine form
Under the cover of darkness is seeking opportunity
Across the unguarded gardens, and planting poisonous seeds; lies
These weeds are voids, black holes in the truth, to be held by this
Illusion
Help me focus my attention to reality which cannot be seen
So I don't make the mistake to accept this weakness
This illusion I see, which I cannot see
Lord, open my eyes!
Power is everything I can make it be
Without my consent, resistance wouldn't be here
So why am I still here?

Faith is freedom. Faith carries us forward. To live a full life, we must have something to believe in, something bigger than ourselves. We are created for a reason; our lives are to serve a specific purpose.

When we believe we have no purpose, we are merely doubting our purpose. But doubt is imprisonment. It holds us back. We become stagnant, chasing momentary pleasures that can never bring the fulfillment that comes with the realization of our life's purpose. This gets us nowhere. It leaves a void that becomes our pain. And when pain has a part in our cause, pain has a part in the effect. We can easily get lost in this world with its distracting enticements and false pleasures.

There is a light you can find to guide you down your path—the right path. God has a unique will for each and every one of our lives. We are created specifically for that reason. We are given gifts, talents, and passions that are to serve this purpose. We may notice these inclinations without giving much thought to them, or we may look over these things altogether. This is why we are given dreams, the visions that reveal to us our purpose. We are even given desires for these visions that promise fulfillment. There are many unknown factors and steps to bringing all of this into manifestation. We must remain aware that there is a source that prepared this path for us. So to seek this source is to seek the escape plan of our spiritual prison. To seek this source is to seek the treasure map to abundant life, the one and only map to our destiny. This is why we must seek God with all our heart, mind, and soul, never wavering. In seeking God, we are pursuing our purpose, finding fulfillment

—It doesn't hurt to pray
There is no pain in that

Humbled

All in my power
I secure this stronghold
Without you
Only putting faith in me
Not that I doubt you
I just don't doubt myself without you
Looking down on me
Trying to look down on you
Not seeing you

Lightning struck my black castle
Its stones became this avalanche
I'm grateful you took me down from my dark mountain
From among shadows that cover me, follow me,
Doing nothing at all for me
Blocking all calls for me
No service here
No servants here
Just gods that never hear,
Gods that I'll never hear
Just gods that tell me what I want to hear,
Gods that I'll never fear

Below me
Places that I can never see
Glory, destiny
I exalted myself
Rising to find a place without direction
There is no direction without a designated place
This I close my mind for
The come up
Here there's a limit
This high place touching the sky
This black night shading starlight
You brought me down

I'm coming down
These highs we always end up chasing
Down
Addiction
To a life without life
A love without love
I can't believe I never fought it now
That inner conflict,
It's like the beloved nagging spouse
I'd hate to leave her my house
That resistance I can't resist
No matter how much your peace insists

Beneath me
I see the entire world
It all seems so small
They all seem so small
From way up here
Perched atop this rigid rock
I see it all
Ignoring the sense this view isn't right
Whispers against loud sights
Howling winds at the top of this cold height
Pushing me
Pushing me to hold on
The pushing that holds me back
That pushes me too far

Then that gravity that pulled me back
It's good to be back

Down to earth

Playing With Him

Playing with my kite
The wind pulls us left and right
Then you pull us to the sky
You pull me so high I feel high
Then you drop me so fast
And I realize I can't fly
I fall so fast, I don't realize I can die
Before I realize I don't die

Playing in my sandbox
You throw dirt in my eyes
I don't see the flood
You drag me through the mud
Where I'm buried alive
Where no one hears my cries

I like to play in the jungle
You abandon me in the wilderness
I wrestle with the wildlife
I'm lost in the current
Swept away by the river
I drown in the ocean

I like to slap box
But you're too fast to fight
You blacken both my eyes
Even though I tell you I'm playing
It seems that makes it worse
You slam me with all your might
You take me down, and fill me with fright
I run, but you yank the back of my shirt as hard as you can
As my collar chokes me, I wonder why I ran
Then you ran me through with your flashing sword
But I would never understand
Without your heavy hand

I Owe You One

Lord, I lust for things I don't have
I betray my needs for what I don't want
Sacrifice for stingy idols
Roast my morals over the fire
The fire of my spirit overcome by the sea of reeds
All for an empty lighter

The truth runs through my veins
So my mind should never idle
Still I open up my heart to closed minds
And let it get stabbed by all those liars
Then I turn my back and let it get stabbed by all those liars

Infinite lies and one truth
How can I not keep up with what's true?
How I love to spend my time, time is money
My love for money is the root of all this evil
I'm hoping that the Lord will sue

Happy with what His will will do
Happy with what will ensue
So happy that I'm humbled now
Still the regret will ooze from my pores
From that stupid mask I used to choose
But happily I hear I lose
Happy that I can't deny
Happy that I'm not confused
Happy just to pay my dues

Although, I still must fret
Because sadly, I'm still in debt

Rededicate

I remember when I left you
At the time it felt like it was what was best to do
At the time, it was the worst for me
I thought it was the best that I could do

But my best is you
My best is left in you
So it got worse for me when I left from you
You were right, I tried to take a left to you
So focused on my half-baked plan
Not thinking of what you may have planned

I ran,
From what I didn't understand
I didn't even understand I ran
I didn't understand
The foreign language of my heart's command
I never heard it speak before
Nor have I heard from it again

Times change again and again
I'm back in the zone again
I feel it once again
You still hold it in your hand
You caress it with your whispers once again
Your lips tender from the elixir of your desires demand
With my mind open, I soak up the potion
And translate the notion
My heart beats with tact, your love back in motion

My life back on track, trained by the facts
I can do bad all by myself
But that doesn't change the fact that I need help
All you wanted to do was help
I tried to help myself, but I can't do it by myself
Unless I want it bad, because I got it bad
Because your love is so good, it . . .
I can't explain
All I can say is, MY GOODNESS!

Faith of Faith

In my mind there's a battle
I tremble from the war when I wake
My heart is too little, my fear is too great
My words are too little to carry the weight
For you to fathom the faith
Which won't shake as earth quakes
And won't break with what breaks
But will take from what takes

I capture the hate
I hang it in faith
It always surrenders too late, I love how it waits
Enemies await
Snares laid in whatever I think
I won't entertain the debate
I know the source of the power
I know what this power creates
I know this won't overcome this strength

Distractions my eyes look above
Whispers drowned in living water
From sponges of living words
Cleaning this plate
The chance to destroy to make way to create
Spiritual food
Attempts to poison this plate
Lies, the thief lies in wait
But my eyes are not on what he says he will take
My love is too great
To love what's at stake

I unload the weight, and go head-on with fate
I don't retreat in its wake
I don't stop, I don't wait
I just watch it create
I just watch me take shape

Fix my face, fix my pace
For the path I must take
For this journey I must make
For victory awaits!

FREE
to avail spirit unrestricted in its fullness of purpose, truth, and identity

Growing

I carry this weight, until it hurts like a motha …
Tears in my face as the pain comes out of me like a motha …
I hurt you, but somehow I still make you smile like a motha …
I don't see the pain, pride got a hold on me like a motha …

I'm blessed like a motha …
I still stress like a motha …
The cries giving me no rest like a motha …
I regret like a motha, then I don't regret like a motha …
The fight is for the best like a motha …

I punish myself like a motha …
But the sun will rise
The sun still looks over the earth
   like a motha …
The rain nurtures what will blossom in the summer
   like a motha …
The storm blows the petals off, but the ground never lets go
   like a motha …
I grow in the struggle like a motha, grow from it like a motha …
Sometimes it gets on my nerves like a motha …
But it always does good for me like a motha …

I can feel it in my words like a motha …
I can feel it like the words of a mother

    Word to my mother

    Words to my mother

What is good for us may not always be good to us (and vice versa). Whatever may come, will come. Optimism isn't merely a hope; it is a technique, a strategy. The vision that sees the way out, to make a way out of no way, working with what we get. At the very least, we might as well enjoy life while what we can't change is happening. Perseverance is the veteran of this battle. Perseverance is a muscle, a muscle that is always being strengthened by this exercise.

—Getting through it by growing from it.

15.

Resolutions
#8962494 #89642984

There is this door
Within a door
If knowledge is power
Wisdom is a force
From experience
Is born a supreme teacher
This omnipresent leader
I mustn't choose to ignore
This knocking . . .
Beyond my deadbolted door

Purpose
What eyes desire
Against a peephole . . .
Naturally a doorway
Moving past a glimpse
To focus on a vision

Open mind

To open minds

Tune into reality. To be immersed in a situation, a description is not an observation. As this narration is more of a ventilation than an explanation, to be concluded as an examination, not a persuasion.

Life teaches through experience, while its host has the opportunity to learn from the outgoing lessons. The teacher is his student in his classroom. For those affected are to be blessed to live by a keen intuition to be more effective. Then the next generation is affected in a greater way to have an even greater affect.

Life's loop will begin an elevation into an infinitely rising spiral. Questions reveal answers that spawn deeper questions. We search to consume the volume of depth itself, in terms of knowledge, to obtain wisdom absolute. We are constantly refining ourselves towards a heightened sense. Decisions will eventually evolve into a default alignment of a sovereign life strategy to behold a superior existence.

This worldly life is a classroom; a university where we only graduate in death. Thus, we must be open, to be present for loved ones as we crossover upon this stage, leaving drying tears as significant memories upon these black threads.

In the Garden

When we hold on to nothing
We must let go for something
I empty my tear ducts
To feed this starving garden
When the drought brings the doubt
When a doubt brings a drought
When we are not prepared
We run out

Hope

To survive
To die alive
I had to make my way
Through
Making use of useless things
I had to recharge my spirit
I had to repair my heart
I had to rewire my mind
But I am no longer the same
I am not fixed,
I am a new creation

Now aware of all truth
I am responsible for self
I am accountable for me
I am in charge of my destiny

I no longer sway like the leaves
I'm the root of the oak
I drink provisions from the heavenlies
I produce exponential growth
The increase

Love was held back
And when it was given it was taken
I starved for such energy
Until I saw why it always left

Until I instilled
Only upon I could I depend
True love which comes from within
To manifest, to produce
The power of the seed

Happiness

They frown when they lose their money
I smile because I had something to lose
I smile because I can get it back
They frown because they don't think of that

They cry when it comes to an end
I anticipate the new beginning
They can't keep their head above water
I just start swimming
They cry when they lose their friends in the tide
I have no problem leaving Wilson
I smile, appreciating the exposed lies
They cry,
No longer being loved
I just learned to love myself
I smile
I'm better at it than anybody else

They hate all the stressin'
I'm in love with the lesson
They're mad that their gun was taken
I'm glad I no longer have to use it
When it's pointed at me
I am at peace
It's only physical pain that I feel

I hear them scream and squeal
And once they get shot they start to cry
But of course I smile
I'm so glad I didn't die

Rain

Falling from the highest place
Caught by the lowest face
We run from it, even though
We need it to grow
All the things it drowns in the flood
All the things that live, that drink, that bud

Miracle in the desert
But you call it bad weather
Someone's pain, someone's pleasure
You wouldn't know pleasure in this way
If you never knew pain
You wouldn't love the sunny days
If you didn't despise the rain

The earth turns too slippery for me to walk in
The dirt turns to mud and I'm stuck
But then it gives moisture to my deprived skin
I'm not really sure how it makes me feel,
If I never knew hurt, I would never know I'd heal
And I'll always thirst
What then, when water bottles come up empty in my search?
I'd look back on the rain and how it came
Looking for where it fell
Puddles to streams to ponds
Things that never fail
And waterfalls make it swell
Water falls making that hole you're in a well
Making it all well

Better Days

I told you there would be better days
I just had to find a better way
You told me that I had to change
Now I have these better ways
Now I can do better things

I told you there would be better days
When you would lay there playing sleep
Rivers leading to stains on your sheets
When you gave up praying for relief
And would just be praying for some sleep

I would stay away from sleep
Scared of what I might see
Things I wish I never had to watch
Watching the clock, hand watching over the glock
Finger nowhere near the trigger
Still eyes are bloodshot
Red lines from constricted dots
Shrinking back from hellish thoughts
Since they say I can't be saved, I run away
I get lost
Now heaven seems too far away
But it seems to be the only way
So I turn around,
And I walk that way

Up all night
Waiting for a better day

But I tell you about these better days
Because they say when the sun comes out it dries up all the rain
And then you see the rain washed away the stains

Those stains, those pains
Those pains that never seem to go away
But if it wasn't for the stains
We wouldn't need the rain
And without the rain, we couldn't appreciate these better days

RESOLUTION
the culmination of perseverance and unwavering determination unto its desired conclusion

Endings

All things come to an end
Hating how good things must reach their endings
Hoping conclusions tie loose ends,
But these new endings just bring us new beginnings

Nothing like an artist in his zone in art
Nothing like being at home in heart
Slightly grieving as it's leaving
But nothing is like a masterpiece in the moment of completion
The rush of the final touch

Nothing like a new start
Blank canvas open for your entry
Nothing like that first stroke
To let go in wonder, where it goes
All these ways to endings of endless
Possibilities

A Note From the Author

I hope this climb through *Growing Pains* has touched your mind, heart, and spirit in some way. Whether encouraging you to look outside your box and above your circumstances, or whether challenging your negative mindframe with positivity, my aim is to lift your spirit. But I'll settle with you knowing that someone can relate to or understand what you are going through.

I thank God for this; I thank God for my savior, Jesus Christ (because the Lord knows I needed saving). I can't forget the Holy Spirit, which led me to this and through this. The way this flowed through me, I am fully convinced it was from God. This is how the title, *Raw Mind*, came about. It was like a download—straight "off the dome" like a freestyle rap—the way these poems and directives were thoughts, but without thought, and without thought became words. I read what I write without knowing where it comes from and then realizing this is exactly how I feel.

I need to get to the people who really matter. Credit to my friends and family for all their belief and encouragement—I'm talking black-card credit. Love for my grandmother, Margie Hall, for investing in this project. For believing in me from day one, along with my amazing mother, Helen Marie, "Miss G," who is still waiting to be put on payroll for all her typing and reading. That is a lot of backpay. That's gonna hurt my pockets, most definitely. My other proofreaders and trusted advisors—Joseph "Tiny Strange" Willis, Xavier "Zay Baby" Killingsworth, Quinton "Alim" Jackson—who helped inspire some of this work and encouraged me in the final stages. Can't forget Lorenzo "Nasr" Fegans who planted the seed that sprouted into the concept of "Diagnosis" and "Prescription"—I know I took it and ran with it, so don't sue me!

I have to thank my amazing editor, Ella Ritchie. This project has evolved so much with your input and our enlightening discussions. Your care for this project and your heart for your craft has made this experience beyond enjoyable and not as stressful as I know it should be—immeasurably more than I could ask or imagine! I know my passion for this has taken a lot of patience. So I definitely want to thank everyone at Stellar Communications Houston for their invaluable work, time, and effort. This would not be anywhere near what it is without such an amazing team.

Thanks also to all I haven't mentioned who know they are worth mentioning for their belief in and encouragement for this vision. I still have this undying desire to impact the world with words in a positive way—to uplift, encourage, and motivate all. My main focus is to bring those who are in a dark place into the light. So, I ask you to continue to follow me in this elevation of consciousness into the next volume, *Soul Searcher*, and beyond if you have a desire in life to reach the Light.

P.S. If you enjoyed *Growing Pains*, please consider leaving an honest review online. Your review allows me to continue sharing my writing.

About the Author

Evan McMillan is a poet who is from Houston, Texas. *Growing Pains* is the first volume of his *RAW MIND* series. McMillan is a born-again Christian striving to grow, leaving his old self behind and finding balance in the life God has designed and desires for him.

In the works
SOUL SEARCHER
Volume II in the *Raw Mind* series

www.ingramcontent.com/pod-product-compliance
Lightning Source LLC
Chambersburg PA
CBHW072149100526
44589CB00015B/2148